ADAM PRICE

WALES: THE FIRST AND FINAL COLONY

D1500885

I Ilar

ADAM PRICE

WALES: THE FIRST AND FINAL COLONY

SPEECHES AND WRITING
2001–2018

First impression: 2018

The publishers wish to acknowledge the support of
Cyngor Llyfrau Cymru

Cover photograph: Keith Morris
Cover design: Y Lolfa

ISBN: 978 1 78461 592 5

Published and printed in Wales
on paper from well-maintained forests by
Y Lolfa Cyf., Talybont, Ceredigion SY24 5HE
website www.ylolfa.com
e-mail ylolfa@ylolfa.com
tel 01970 832 304
fax 832 782

Contents

Acknowledgements 7

Foreword (by Cynog Dafis) 9

1 This is our moment 13

2 A wealthy country that 24
lives in poverty (Part 1)

3 Wales, the first and final colony 29

4 We are the ones we've been waiting for 54

5 When Adam got in for Carmarthen 64

6 High crimes and misdemeanours 70

7 We fought a war over an arsenal 74
of non-existent weapons

8 A bittersweet farewell 83

9 Declaration of Independence 85

10 Democratic deficit 88

11 The red-green grass of home: 92
in support of a Plaid / Labour alliance

12 Democratic socialism and the people 95

13 Reinventing radical Wales 97

14 Changing the course of a nation 115

15 Labour is now Robin Hood in reverse 121

16 We must own our own mistakes   130
    and our own solutions

17 That temporary Parliament   139
    on the banks of the Thames

18 *A fo ben, bid bont* – Let he (or she)   150
    that would be leader, be a bridge

19 Ammanford's egghead   152

20 Why we need devolution in reverse   154

21 The glacial speed of Welsh progress   158

22 It's good to be home   161

23 There is nothing wrong with   168
    Wales that Wales cannot put right

24 A new dynamic: rising to the   176
    challenge of change

25 This year of serial disappointments   187
    will not extinguish our hope

26 A new Wales, a new chance   194

27 A Guggenheim for Wales   200

28 A penny on tax will help   206
    wake Welsh potential

29 In politics, momentum is everything   209

30 A wealthy country that lives   213
    in poverty (Part 2)

Acknowledgements

THIS BOOK BRINGS together selected speeches and writing which spans two decades, two Parliaments and two Continents, and one political life, in at least its opening chapters.

Listing the people that have helped give me a platform to share my ideas and develop my thinking over this period would need a separate publication in itself. But I should like to give special mention to a few if I may: to my parents, Angela and Rufus, who first gave me the confidence to speak; to Kevin Morgan, who gave me my first job and helped me find my voice; to the fellow members of Plaid Cymru, who, though I now carry the title of Leader, have been not so much a party but more a family to me, in their affection and encouragement; to the people of the communities of my home constituency, Carmarthen East and Dinefwr, who elected me their tribune not once, but twice – an ultimate honour but also the deepest responsibility; and to my predecessor and successor in each role, Rhodri Glyn Thomas and Jonathan Edwards. I should also like to thank the sustaining circle of love that my family and friends have been, chief among them my partner and our newborn son, to whom this book is dedicated.

In relation to this publication itself I should like to thank the publishers Y Lolfa, particularly Lefi Gruffudd and Fflur Arwel for seeing the initial potential, and Carolyn Hodges for bringing it to fruition; Ioan Roberts for his skilful work in editing a volume which could have been several times as long, though considerably less readable; John Osmond for his expert assistance in proofreading at considerable speed and

7

his – as ever – prescient suggestions; my brother, Adrian, for his historical expertise, Ceri Sherlock and Steffan Bryn for their unstinting friendship and unique insight; Carl Harris for general encouragement and support; and finally Cynog Dafis for his magnificent Foreword, his artful Welsh translation and three decades' worth of advocacy and advice.

Diolch o galon i chi i gyd.

Adam Price
November 2018

Foreword

Cometh the hour, cometh the man, cometh the book

THE PUBLICATION OF *Wales: The First and Final Colony*, soon to be launched in all corners of the country, is perfectly timed. Product of two decades of political-activist thought and in preparation since before this year's leadership campaign, it is now placed in our hands at the time when Plaid Cymru seeks to transform itself, expand its membership and support, and gird its loins for the 2021 election campaign, after which it fully intends to form a new Welsh Government. The timing and sequencing is unmistakeably Adam.

The content of these speeches and essays – passionate, eloquent, analytical, inspirational – provided the raw material of Adam Price's leadership campaign and now indicates clearly the direction in which he wishes to lead his party and the vision he has for a new Wales. So if you want to know what Adam Price is about (politically, I mean), you need to read this book. Equally, as Adam was elected with an unmistakeable mandate (64% of the party's vote), if you want to know what Plaid Cymru is going to be about for the foreseeable future, you'd better study and digest this book.

In one sense, of course, Plaid Cymru will still be what it has always been. Not for the first time, I have been struck

9

by the similarity between Adam and Gwynfor: respresenting pretty much the same constituency; their roots in evangelical Christianity; respectful of the Wales that is and has been and committed to the vastly different Wales that is to be; the appeal to history; internationalist in reference and outlook.

Look at the truly magisterial chapter here, 'Wales, the first and final colony', to be seen perhaps as the foundation stone of Adam's nationalist philosophy. It is his *Aros Mae*. Having once read it – evidentially striking, analytically searching – who dare quibble about the claim that Wales was for centuries a colony (first external and then internal) and that it bears the scars, constitutional, political, economic and cultural, to this very day? It is also a brilliant commentary on colonialism itself, in all its baleful manifestations.

But Adam is not just a reincarnated Gwynfor. To begin with, the context is different. For both of them, Wales is a nation of limitless potential inhibited through its absorption by its powerful neighbour into a centralised, conformist state: in Adam's words, 'a wealthy country that lives in poverty'. For Gwynfor there was only one solution: self-government. For Adam, likewise, the constitutional question (independence) is fundamental, but he operates in a Wales that has already achieved a significant measure of self-government. What bugs him is that the potential of this partially self-governing Wales will by 2021 have been stifled for 23 years in the embrace of a Labour-dominated one-party state. "Labour in Wales is failing, and it will fail," he says, and it is Plaid Cymru that must "pick up the pieces".

So Plaid simply *must* win in 2021, not because it seeks power for its own sake, but to put in place a 10-year programme of national transformation, setting in motion also an informed national conversation on Wales' constitutional status, culminating in a referendum on independence – bearing in mind that Scotland may well by then be independent and Ireland on its way to unification.

Note the sequencing. This is not old-fashioned "everything will be great when we're independent" stuff. This is about national transformation as a precondition of independence. In this process Policy, based on innovative, radical, out-of-the-box ideas, is queen.

And here is another difference from Gwynfor. Adam is an economist and no mean technocrat, as well as a visionary. Hence his long-thought-through ten-year plan to "close Offa's Gap". Freeing ourselves from dependence on the not-so-munificent UK Treasury is essential, politically, economically and psychologically. Economics (green and sustainable, of course, bearing in mind the central crisis of our time) moves centre stage.

At this point, enter entrepreneurialism. Here is a politician deeply embedded in Welsh socialism who respects and values enterprise. Adam is unequivocally committed to the redistribution of wealth in favour of the poor. However, that in itself is not enough. We must indeed seek to create a "sound economic life in which great discrepancies cannot occur", but we also need a "new dynamic, a new synthesis between the social democratic values of old and the enterprise, innovation and creativity of a new generation".

Finally, we have in the chapter significantly entitled 'A new dynamic: rising to the challenge of change' a merciless exposé of the deficiencies of current governance and a recipe for fundamental reform. You cannot implement a coherent transformational policy programme, Adam is saying, unless your public service is fit for purpose, culturally as much as structurally. This is a First Minister-in-waiting who knows the score and intends to hit the ground running.

In conclusion, I must briefly mention only some of the other characteristics that make Adam Price a politician of note: a highly absorbent and retentive, as well as penetrating, intellect; mastery of language and impressive literary skills; culture both rooted and cosmopolitan; an extraordinary range of knowledge and reference. Personally he has every reason to be supremely self-confident but seems to be not in the least bit conceited. He listens well, pays careful attention to advice and appreciates no end the efforts of his supporters and predecessors. In his father Rufus' words to me, "Adam is genuine". Yet he can be devastating in his assaults on political opponents.

Recalling the opening words of this preface, then, my humble address to Plaid Cymru and the people of Wales would run as follows:

Recognise that now is the Hour

Support (in every sense) the Man and his mission

Buy, study and share his Book.

Cynog Dafis
November 2018

1

This is our moment

Plaid Cymru Autumn Conference, Cardigan – 2018

'WELSH POLITICS IS coming alive again'... that's probably one of the most unlikely headlines ever in the 87-year history of *GQ* magazine. But we're grateful nevertheless, because they're right. There is something happening in Wales. We are at a crossroads as a country. And I don't mean Britain in Europe; I mean Wales in Europe and Wales in the world, Wales in our heart and Wales in our mind. A hinge-point in our history.

One path forward is the same path as our past.

1918 marks not just the centenary of the end of the First World War but also the beginning of a hundred years of Labour's rule in Wales. That great Party, once a movement, a force for change, has shrivelled into the management class of the status quo, shackling us to the corpse of a British body politic which in all its pathetic machinations these days is doing a pretty convincing impersonation of the last days of the Austro-Hungarian empire. If chucking Chequers is on the agenda, can we please ditch Downing Street too?

For twenty years, what passes for political leadership in Wales has failed the test of our times. Welsh politics has been an oasis of stasis in a sea-full of change. And politics abhors a vacuum every bit as much as nature. So many of our people have begun to lose faith in democracy, hope in the future and belief in themselves. Some have cheered on Brexit as enthusiastically as the crowds a hundred years ago cheered on those marching to the Somme. But now as then, as the dream of Empire sours, the Welsh nation, an even more ancient nation, begins to rouse from its long slumber. There is something happening in Wales. And it's us. These moments, when history speeds up, when minds and hearts open up, when a nation begins to rise up, come along just once a generation. This is our moment. This is our time. This is our chance.

Now, in times such as these the first imperative is to be unambiguous. We have to be honest with the people of our country. There is no sustainable solution to the problems and challenges we face without Welsh independence. It's only by owning our own problems that we will solve them, by owning our own opportunities that we will seize them, by owning our own dream – not Boris Johnson's, not Jacob Rees-Mogg's or Jeremy Corbyn's – that we will ever turn our Welsh dreams into our Welsh reality. And we have to be honest with our people about the destructive potential of a brittle, bitter Brexit.

Some argue there is a contradiction in arguing for Europe and for Welsh independence. But for this nation, Wales and Europe have always been tightly woven together like a Celtic knot, from the thousand words of Latin in our language to our roots in a Celtic civilisation that once ranged from Turkish Galatia to our own *Pays de Galles*. We may be the descendants of the original Britons, but we Welsh were always Romano-Britons, a hybrid culture that looks outward, not just inward, and to the future, not just to someone else's manufactured past.

When England's kings sought to crush our independence 600 years ago, it was envoys from Scotland, France and Castile that honoured us with their presence when Glyndŵr became our Prince. And in 1415, a few years after he had disappeared, there was a Council of Christendom, the European Parliament of its day. There, as Gwyn Alf Williams pointed out, an English delegate proposed that voting should be by nation, not diocese. It was a French delegate who stood up to argue that the Welsh on the island of Britain were not part of the English nation, that we were a nation in our own right. It was by a European in a European Parliament that we were first proclaimed as a nation to the world. You did not forget us then, and we will not forget you now.

In 1979 a referendum to establish a Welsh Assembly was lost. It took almost twenty years for that mistake to be overturned with another referendum. We cannot wait twenty years to undo the damage that is about to befall us. To see our farming industry decimated, our fishing sector eliminated, our manufacturing base eviscerated. Brexit poses the greatest existential threat of our generation to the agricultural sector as a whole and to upland family farms in particular.

Mirroring Michael Gove, the Labour Welsh Government's response to this is proposing to take away the farmers' safety net by phasing out the Basic Payment Scheme from 2020. In Wales, 80% of an average farmer's income comes from the Common Agricultural Policy, and this figure is likely to be even higher in Wales' uplands. Wales is 4.7% of the UK population, but receives over 9% of EU funds that come to the UK. Meanwhile, our principal competitors in the European Union will continue to take over 70% of Common Agricultural Policy support as direct payments. The Scottish Government is maintaining basic payments. Northern Ireland will do so as well. Even Labour's shadow DEFRA Secretary, Sue Hayman, has announced that Labour in England would maintain basic farm payments. This is creating an uneven playing field for Wales.

The FUW has spent the summer arguing strongly that the Welsh Government's proposals would be the biggest change since the Second World War to agriculture in Wales. Despite this, very little modelling has been done on the effects of this drastic policy change. The proposals, particularly in relation to doing away with basic payments to farmers, could do to our rural communities what Margaret Thatcher did to industrial communities in Wales. We've heard about the Highland Clearances in Scotland; if we are looking at family farms going out of business, then it will be the upland clearances of Wales. Plaid Cymru believes that all farmers should continue to receive a basic income. Any new system following Brexit must give direct support to active farmers rather than rewarding land ownership in itself.

But it's not just rural Wales that is facing catastrophe. We're on the *Titanic*'s deck. The iceberg's looming. The Government's strategy is to tell the iceberg to move. Those in first class have taken to the lifeboats – David Cameron's on a beach somewhere, Jacob Rees Mogg's firm has moved to Dublin. The people that are left are locked in the third-class cabins. We have got to break that deadlock. We need to give people a chance and a choice to avert a disaster, for it is they that will pay the heaviest price. Which is why we say it is time for a people's vote.

But what is Labour doing in all this? Holding hands with Theresa May as the band plays *Nearer My God to Thee*. We lost the vote in the National Assembly because Labour and the Liberal Democrat – I have to use the singular – couldn't bring themselves to vote for it. Like Brexit itself, Labour under Corbyn promises the illusion of change. But for us in Wales, Labour represents the very essence of the politics of the past; which is why we must become the party of tomorrow.

That's the crossroads that we face. That's the choice. Change versus more of the same. The future or the past. The Old Wales or the New Wales. To build the New Wales, we must invest in the next generation. Wales should be the best place in the world in which to be young. This starts at the beginning of a child's life.

The Lib Dems in 2015 proposed that free school meals should be available to all primary school children in England, but Kirsty Williams and Welsh Labour in Government are doing quite the opposite. Due to their decision to cap the eligibility of families on Universal Credit for free school meals at a net earned income of £7,400, more than 40% of children who live in poverty in Wales will not be eligible for free school meals. This will be the least generous offer in the UK, as *all* children in early years education in Scotland and England are provided with free school meals. Meanwhile the cap for earned income in Northern Ireland has been set at £14,000 – almost double the level proposed in Wales.

Childcare costs Welsh families nearly a quarter of their income, even before tax. The Labour Welsh Government's childcare offer provides families earning up to £200,000 a year with thirty hours a week of free childcare for three year olds, but does not provide this to parents seeking work or who are in education or training. So much for Labour's 'Flying Start' – more a flailing start. Shame on them. It's time for a new start for Wales. A Plaid Cymru government that I lead will deliver a comprehensive child package, making it possible for parents to return to work when they choose and giving children from all backgrounds a good start in life with a healthy nutritious meal, clothes for school, support to attend field trips and receive a world-class education. That's how we win a New Wales.

But to build those new foundations – of confidence, promise and prosperity – we must renew ourselves as a party. New ideas. New ways of thinking. New ways of working. Over the course of the leadership election I outlined my desire to transform our Party into an election-winning machine. What became clear to me this summer is that members across the country, those of you who have given years of selfless service to the Party, also shared this aim. We have pockets of success. Where we are well established, we have Plaid Cymru community councillors, county councillors, Assembly Member, Member of Parliament, Police and Crime Commissioner and Plaid-run Council. In other constituencies, our candidates are often the agent, leaflet designer, press officer, organiser and canvasser too. If we are to win, we need to transform. We have to turn supporters into members and members into activists. We must expand our campaign resources in every sense.

We will re-establish a National Campaigns Unit to deliver a dedicated team of support campaigns across the country. It will consist of specialists in communications and strategy. It will pilot and roll out cutting-edge campaign technologies, and provide all the services you need to succeed.

Alongside this will be a National Organising Academy to support our volunteers to become leaders in their community and teach the principles of grassroots organising. It will support candidates, branches and constituencies with their local plans to achieve positive change in their areas. From the local 'Save our School' campaign to standing for Parliament, organising and expanding the group of grassroots activists through building personal relationships with voters will be crucial to achieving a Plaid Cymru government in 2021.

To make sure we get this right, we need a full and honest assessment of where we're at. I am therefore pleased to announce that my first act as Leader of the Party was to commission the former SNP Westminster Leader and coordinator of the SNP's independence campaign, Angus Robertson, to conduct a root-and-branch review of the Party's campaign machinery. This will look at our structures, our operations, capacity and ability to secure victory for Plaid Cymru in every corner of the country.

In their desperate attempts to divert attention away from the Brexit splits, both Labour and the Tories are cynically calling for snap elections in Wales and Westminster. My message to them today is that Plaid Cymru will have an election-winning machine ready to face the challenge whenever an election comes, so bring it on. Let the battle begin. A battle between the old ideas, new ideas and no ideas. We will succeed as the party of the new ideas, of the new Wales, of the new horizon. The modernisers of an ancient nation.

With leadership elections in each of the political parties, this should be a Great Reset moment in Welsh politics, a political renaissance. But when the new Welsh Conservative leader Paul Davies was challenged to mention a single new policy on BBC Wales' *Wales Live,* he couldn't even come up with one. In the old unionist parties, the cupboard is bare. Theirs is a desert of inspiration in a nation that is thirsting for change. Welsh Labour's Carwyn Jones, like the late Rhodri Morgan before him, has been a great communicator who has talked the talk, but without saying or doing anything of any substance. They were great at holding court. But what Wales needs is not a monarch but a prime minister, with the vision and the knowledge and the ideas to translate into action.

We want Wales to be a creative country, a knowledge nation, a land of innovation, of inspiration and of hope. The hope that unites humanity, that sustains us all through dark times, that is the focus of our love for each other and for each new generation. The hope that the future will be better than the past, that the hopes and the dreams of all the years will not have been in vain, that we will persevere and that we will prevail, that we will win the new world and the new Wales for which we have yearned for so long.

That new Wales is on the horizon. Its shores are beckoning. It's time for us to be like Bendigeidfran, be the bridge that gets us there. We must fire up the national imagination with a sense of the Wales that might be. We must create in our people a realisation of the radical urgency of now. A realisation that we cannot afford to keep doing what we have done for another five years. That it's time to end the well-worn path of decline – the disgrace of falling life expectancy, the scandal of the collapse in educational rankings, the ignominy of the 'sick man of Europe' status of our economy – and instead begin to chart a new course.

We have been a nation of innovators. When the Welsh armies at the Battle of Crug Mawr here in Cardigan faced the superior forces of the Anglo-Norman invaders, seeking to turn

19

us into a vassal state – you see, there is nothing novel in this year's Westminster power grab – what did they do but innovate? And so the longbow, which was to dominate Europe until the invention of gunpowder, was invented here. The weapon of a David confronted with Goliath.

But we have been a nation of innovators in saving lives too. It was David Lloyd George who introduced the first social insurance scheme for health in 1911. It was Emily Talbot of Port Talbot who endowed the first full-time public health chair in preventative medicine in the world in Cardiff in 1917. In 1948, of course, Aneurin Bevan introduced the NHS – the Tredegarisation of the whole country, the first system to offer free medical care to the whole population anywhere in the world. In 1972 evidence-based medicine began building on Archie Cochrane and Iain Chalmers' work in the south Wales Valleys. Following on from Cochrane's work, Chalmers founded the Cochrane Collaboration, which is credited with preventing millions of deaths and disabilities.

But this spirit of innovation has come shuddering to a halt. We have seen the default thinking at play in the Welsh Government's budget this week. How does the Welsh Government make its budget? Well, I've seen them up close enough to make my mind up now. There is no strategic thinking. They start by raising everyone's budget or more often cutting everything by a standard amount – and then the Health Service gets more because it is in crisis, so everyone else gets a haircut. And social care therefore gets cut, which means an even bigger crisis in the Health Service the following year. But the truth is that no amount of new money will solve our Health Service problems if unaccompanied by new thinking. We spend 40% of our entire national budget on the Health Service, and the OECD says that about 20% of that makes no or minimal contribution to good health outcomes. Worse than that, data from Wales and other countries shows that about one in ten patients are actually harmed by hospital admission.

I want us to develop a comprehensive new vision for health and care. Work is already underway, being led by Dr Dai Lloyd. I want this approach to every area of public policy. That is why I will be setting up a series of panels – each of which will be provided with terms of reference, priorities and a direction of travel. For health these will be:

- The creation of a National Care Service alongside the NHS.

- A shift in emphasis from hospital-based to GP-led primary-care health provision in the community.

- A One Health approach which integrates health not just with care but with housing, education, transport, food and the environment.

We'll ask the panel also to examine the four compromises made by Aneurin Bevan:

- Continued private practice by consultant specialists.

- The continued status of GPs as private operators of public service.

- The second-tier status of areas like mental and public health.

- The absence of local democratic accountability.

We can and will go further even than Bevan – and build the truly universal health and care service of which he could only dream. We want to embrace that spirit of radical and transformational thinking in every area of Welsh life. We are not here to reproduce the past, tinker at the edges, or slavishly accept the current paradigm of conventional thinking. We are here to remake Wales and fashion it into a beacon of what the world could become. We want Wales to be the world's test bed. As Phil Williams used to say, we are the perfect scale for innovation: big enough to matter, small enough to manage – a nation of natural co-operators, with one degree of separation, not six.

When I'm First Minister, we'll re-localise the economy, watering the roots and building up the foundations. We'll do what the French Government has done and guarantee by law that at least 50% of food bought by the public sector is local.

When I'm First Minister, we'll make up for generations of under-investment by leapfrogging and building the future here – building a reliable, fast, modern, renewably powered National Western Rail Line for Wales, linking Swansea with Bangor. We don't need your Western Powerhouse, Mr Cairns – we'll build our own here in Wales.

When I'm First Minister, we'll create a real Development Bank to offer loans to help local companies grow and, when necessary, to be bought by the staff to help companies made in Wales stay in Wales and prosper.

When I'm First Minister, we'll create a Welsh national energy company, with the profit used to build up a basic income for all our citizens. Governing as if we are already independent, we'll build the confidence to get there.

Of course I can achieve none of this on my own. We have a mountain to move and each of us must grab a shovel. There is no 'I' in Wales. There is a 'We'. We need everyone who cares about Wales to help build this new Wales, whether you're a member of Plaid or not, whether you're a supporter of any party or none. We can't do this without you. Join us. And that's why I'm pleased to tell you that the Party has agreed to waive the membership fee for those who sign up to the Party over the coming weeks. Indeed, one person who has joined us this week is Grenville Ham, the former leader of the Green Party in Wales. Passion, purpose, knowledge and innovation define Grenville as a person, and they define what we must become as a party. What is this Party, after all? What have we ever been but a wake-up call to the nation? If what we do remains the same, then so will what we are. The arc of history is not a straight line. We have to bend it to our purpose, like those longbows at Crug Mawr. This is our moment of change. History is in our hands. We can make it if we choose.

During my sabbatical from front-line politics at the Kennedy School in Harvard, one of John F Kennedy's most famous lines about going to Washington stuck in my mind: "the thing that surprised me the most was that things were as bad as we said they were." That's how I feel every day at the Assembly, and I don't want to feel that way a day longer than I have to. When we look at the Wales that is, it can be heart-breaking. But I joined this Party – and you joined this cause – because we don't settle for the Wales that is, we strive for what might be.

That Wales is waiting. It's waiting for us. There is no *Mab* or *Merch Darogan*, no Son or Daughter of Prophecy. This is about us. We are the ones we have been waiting for. And this is the moment we have been waiting for, all our political lives. We must become the hope of those without hope, the disillusioned, the disenfranchised. Those who believe they cannot achieve their dreams; who have been sold a deceitful and undeliverable dream; who believe we cannot ever become the Wales we need to be.

Our message to the Welsh people must be simple: *Yes, Wales Can.* We can be prosperous. We can be confident. We can be fair and flourishing. We can be self-governing and successful. We can be Welsh and European. We can be independent and we can get there sooner than you think. This is our chance to turn the page on the politics of the past. Our opportunity to bring new energy and new ideas to the problems we face, to offer a new direction and a new dynamic to the country that we love. Our time to write a new chapter in Wales' story.

It will not be written for us in the marbled halls of Whitehall and Westminster. It will be written by us in the streets and shops, the pubs and clubs, the homes and hearts of our nation. And it starts and it ends with us. If we hope for a better Wales, then we must begin to believe we can get there. If we begin to believe, then we can and we will, because our time for change has come. We are on our way – we can't wait another day. Together we can build the country we know we can be. *Gyda'n gilydd gallwn ennill Cymru Newydd.* Together we can win a New Wales.

2

A wealthy country that lives in poverty (Part 1)

Plaid Cymru Spring Conference, Llangollen – 2018

WE ARE 19 months away from the beginning of a new decade. New decades are, by definition, a time of new departures. And this new decade will certainly be that, starting with the *terra incognita* of Brexit, bequeathed as a legacy by the decision from the previous decade. But new decades also bring with them the sense of new possibility, new potential and new hope.

This decade more than most contains within it the seeds of Great Transformation. It will be the age of automation, a second machine age – even perhaps an age of abundance to follow our own age of austerity. It will be a new Electric Age in the wake of Peak Oil. And for those of us old enough to remember getting the keys to our own front door at 21, it will be the decade at the beginning of which our Parliament – and it will be a Parliament – will finally come of age.

It's ends of decades from the late 1960s to the late 1990s that have been the hinge points of history, marking the dawning of a new age. Though sometimes that new age – as in 1979 – is stillborn. For there is never any inevitability about the future: whether it carries us on its crested waves to sunlit pastures, or crashes our hopes against the storm-gates of destiny, depends on the choices we make in the final phase of each decade. For while we, as Welsh Nationalists, cannot choose our geography or our history, the weather – alas, I mean this only in the symbolic sense – we can make our own.

Now, the first point in moving forward is always looking back. I sound like a driving instructor, not a political leader! But in politics, as in the Highway Code, checking your mirrors is always a good way to start. It's those who went before us that will often show us the path ahead. So today I give you Hywel Stanford Hughes, who almost 90 years ago hosted the first ever Urdd camp at his home here in Llangollen.

The son of a Methodist minister, he left Wales in 1907 for Bogota, as you do, and soon displayed considerable business acumen, acquiring 27,000 acres which he developed for cattle rearing, expanding his interests into coffee, agricultural machinery, oil and cattle breeding, and soon establishing an office in New York. He was an enthusiastic lifelong member and benefactor of this Party and was probably the only rancher ever inducted into the Gorsedd of Bards, under the name Don Hywel. His entry in the *Dictionary of Welsh Biography* ends with this wonderful encapsulation: "His aspirations may be summarised: to improve the standard of cattle breeding generally and to seek independence for Wales." *Diolch*, Don Hywel for your aspiration, your inspiration and your determination.

The story of Hywel Stanford Hughes gives the lie to one of the most pernicious myths about the Welsh nation: that we somehow lack an entrepreneurial flair. That we are a passive nation congenitally condemned to poverty. So let us first restate something that should be obvious. There is nothing inevitable about Welsh poverty. It is man-made and what is man-made can be undone.

And let us tackle that other myth, for Wales is not a poor nation. In per capita income, in current dollar terms, we're richer than every nation in Asia bar two, every nation in the Americas bar two, and richer than more than half of Europe. Richer than the super-powers of Russia and China – and we've beaten both in soccer, of course. Richer than Slovenia, than South Korea and Spain. Richer than oil-rich Saudi Arabia, Kuwait and Bahrain in the Gulf and the offshore havens of Bermuda and the Bahamas in the Caribbean. We are among the top 30 richest nations on the planet. As such, we would be automatic members of the world's club of high-income countries, the OECD.

We are a wealthy country whose people live in poverty, and therein lies the tragedy of modern Wales, from the kindling sparks of the industrial revolution which this country fired to the successful but suffering country that we still are today. So let us reflect on the seven scourges of contemporary Wales.

- On health we have, for example, the second-lowest survival rate in lung cancer in the EU after Bulgaria. We have the lowest number of doctors per head of any country in the EU after that country, Poland and Romania.

- Of the four nations in these islands, at 23% we have the highest proportion living in poverty. That's over 700,000 of our people in poverty, both absolute and relative; 185,000 of them children.

- With average house prices at almost six times the average wage, we have among the least affordable housing of any country in the world – and the slowest growing housing stock of any nation in the UK.

- In education, in the 2015 PISA tests, Wales – for the fourth time – ranked the lowest of all the UK nations. Of the 70 countries which took part, Wales ranked 36th for maths, 38th for reading and 33rd for science. In other words, we are doing worse educationally than economically, which does not bode well for the future.

- On productivity, we have the lowest average productivity figure in the UK, and we have fallen further behind since the onset of devolution.

- Our infrastructure reflects our colonial past. No other modern developed nation lacks both decent rail and road links between the north and south of its country. And no other country which is itself an electricity exporter lacks a national electricity grid to meet the demands of its own businesses. There are businesses in Wales that cannot expand, that cannot create jobs – though the market is there for them – simply because there is not the capacity in the electricity grid. And that nineteenth-century problem for a twenty-first-century nation is reflected in exactly the same way in the scandalous broadband situation. If Cornwall can have 32% full fibre to its premises, then why is Wales languishing on a mere 4.6%?

- And then we come to what some would say is the biggest scourge of all. The fact that 83% of our country's children leave secondary education without fluency in their own national language, and that less than two thirds of our nation's citizens now identify themselves as Welsh at all.

The paradox of Wales is that we are a rich country, in both material and non-material terms, which has been condemned to poverty of circumstance and of ambition; a rich country that has learned to be poor with a legacy of sickness, under-achievement, under-investment and a lack of self-confidence in our very existence as a nation. British rule in Wales has left deep scars. By and large it has not been tyrannical, but it has been grossly negligent, and left us without the necessary tools with which to achieve our potential as a nation. Unless we free ourselves from the dead hand of London, then we will never get anywhere as a country and as a people.

I was reminded of this slightly comically recently when I made the short walk from Tŷ Hywel to that neo-colonial outpost, the Wales Office on Caspian Way. In that part of Cardiff things tend to be named after references to children's literature: for example, Roald Dahl Plass. In this case it was C S Lewis and Narnia. And as I pressed the security intercom and a disembodied voice in clipped anglophone tones intoned, "How can I help you?", I felt a little bit like the faun in *The Lion, the Witch and the Wardrobe*, about to be turned into stone.

I was there to see the secret Brexit impact assessment. Written by civil servants paid for by Wales' taxes about the country in which we live, it was a document I could read but I couldn't take with me or show to the people that elected me, though I could write the whole thing out in longhand. Before I started, they got out a small lined metal container which I thought initially was Alun Cairns' daybed, but was actually a safe-deposit box for my mobile phone. For those few moments I was in a parallel world: a spy from the future, an ambassador of a free Wales with special diplomatic immunity, visiting the Snow Queen's icy lair. I made my excuses and returned to my country through the nearest fur coat.

You know, if you suffer one of those moments of existential angst that Aneurin Bevan used to call "the invasion of doubt" and ask whether your place is in this Party, then remind yourself one by one of each of those seven scourges. The premature deaths, the lives blighted by poverty and poor skills, this dislocated nation that has all the potential but none of the levers to succeed.

I don't think it will be long before that doubt is well and truly banished. Wales cannot afford our doubt – it desperately needs our determination. Nevertheless, we will not build up this nation through grieving for the things we lack. Self-pity is the world's worst motivator. We've comforted ourselves too long by blaming others for our misfortunes. The answer is to take our future into our own hands...

3

Wales, the first and final colony

Institute of Welsh Politics Annual Address, Aberystwyth – November 2009

HISTORY DOES NOT repeat itself, but it sure does rhyme, said Mark Twain. So it is that Wales, for much of its history an anomaly, today finds itself anomalous again. Before the Act of Union, we were a conquered nation that was never fully subdued. Post-devolution, we're a post-colonial country still waiting to be decolonised. It is these contradictions that describe our present predicament: we are a hybrid state living in the cracks between a dependent past and an independent future.

This lecture is unabashedly didactic. It hopes to convince you of three propositions no less revolutionary for all their simplicity: that the *longue durée* of English imperialism began here in Wales; that the deepest legacy it has left is psychological; and that national liberation, if it is to mean anything, has to be a liberation of the mind. Otherwise we will be condemning ourselves to be not just the first but also the final colony.

To begin at the beginning: English imperialism can perhaps

be described as Wales' greatest and most terrible export. What was tried and tested here soon became the template for what one English historian has called the "thousand-year Reich" of the English empire. It is a pedigree we appear to have worked very hard to forget. The title of 'First Colony' is a crown of thorns more often claimed by the Irish – most recently in setting the scene for the 2005 BBC series *This Sceptred Isle*, which focused on Empire. And yet the Normans settled Wales nearly a century before Ireland, and the Statute of Rhuddlan, formally annexing Wales, predates its Irish equivalent, the Statute of Kilkenny, by about the same number of years. Whatever the Irish suffered, we sadly suffered first.

A plausible case for English colonialism's origins could perhaps be made by the Cornish. But Cornwall was merged with Wessex before England as a nation proper had been formed. So though it may be the great unspoken fact of our identity, we in Wales were indeed the first piece in England's empire.

But does enough of our past qualify as colonial in the classical sense for this to have relevance for us today?

Answering that question means looking in turn at each of the six core features of colonialism: military conquest, settlement, cultural assimilation, political subjugation, economic exploitation and racial discrimination. There is plenty of evidence of all of them at work in Wales over the best part of a millennium, but the most obvious and least debatable is the brutal fact of the conquest itself: Even today, Edward I's ring of iron stands as a potent reminder of our colonial past. The Normans' castle building programme in Wales remains the most concerted effort at the pacification of an occupied country in European history.

Of course, Wales was to prove, in that classic formulation, an easier country to conquer than to hold. England's new rulers quickly extended their control of the river valleys and coastal lowlands seasonally vacated by a farming people that in the summer moved their stock to the hills. In some important sense, they never conquered Wales above six hundred feet, where their heavily armoured knights lost their advantage over Welsh archers and lightly armed infantry. Indeed the "piecemeal, long-drawn out and uncompleted" nature of the English conquest of Wales was the reason it had to be done again and again. The highlands and the forests remained in the hands of a Welsh insurgency using the tactics of guerrilla warfare as described by that mixed-race Cambro-Norman Gerald of Wales. Between 1090 and 1415 Wales was a country in rebellion or else under siege, raiding or being raided, celebrating victory or coping with defeat. The landscape for the English occupying power was as hospitable as Helmand.

But the Norman conquest was no mere military affair. Territorial annexation by force was simply the prelude to the entire panoply of measures in colonialism's armoury. First came the movement into Wales of whole populations of English or Flemings, combined with the forced displacement of the indigenous Welsh. Wales was divided into two separate domains: 'Englishries' and 'Welshries', a powerful settler minority and a conquered native populace. This was not the natural, organic shift of population happening all over Europe throughout the Middle Ages. This was a deliberate act of state policy that presaged the creation of 'Planter' settlements elsewhere in the tragic unfolding story of colonialism.

Alongside their castelries, the Anglo-Norman invaders created in Wales a powerful bulwark in the chartered town with borough status. A class of special liberties – the so-called Laws of Breteuil, imported from that Normandy town by the Marcher Lords – was created to entice settlers in as surely as the castle was designed to keep the Welsh out. While Carmarthen, Montgomery and even Aberystwyth were soon sites of growth for a nascent property-owning English merchant class, the Welsh became outcasts, confined to the favelas of medieval Wales on the margins of town or in the rural uplands. In this way, the Welsh are not just the original inhabitants of these islands. They are also the very first to be socially excluded.

The third vector of colonialism is cultural: the supplanting of 'inferior' local languages and traditions by the supposedly superior culture of the colonial power. The first stage, after all, of any sustained colonial project is to convince oneself that conquest is 'ordained of God' and necessary for the 'civilisation' of a barbarous people. The first victim was a slightly anarchic Celtic church, soon Romanised into an orderly hierarchy of bishoprics and parishes all under the ultimate authority of the state-approved denizen of the Canterbury see.

Ecclesiastical colonialism is the first of the great continuities of Welsh history as it features in all three waves of colonial conquest: Norman, Tudor and Victorian. So in the early years of the Norman occupation, we have the sidelining of ancient abbeys dedicated to the names of Welsh holy men by local Benedictine franchises – the religious equivalent of Starbucks or McDonalds – promoting universal saints with no local connection. With Cistercian support, Wales was able to rebuild aspects of a national church in the thirteenth century, an achievement that Glyndŵr sought to consolidate through the programme agreed at the Pennal Synod. With that dream defeated, the English delegate at the Council of Constance was able to declare when the issue of the Welsh church was raised: *"inclytanatio Anglicana Brytannica"*, an early Latin rendition of "For Wales, see England".

Fast-forward five centuries and in the second wave of colonisation – closely tied as it was to the Reformation of Convenience under Henry VIII – we have a state-funded campaign of iconoclasm targeting such medieval shrines and images of Welsh piety as Derfel Fawr, St Winifred's Well, our Lady of Cardigan and the Virgin of Penrhys. The English Bishop of St Davids hates the cult of St David so much that he strips the lead off the roof of the Cathedral and moves the Bishop's Palace to Abergwili, where it remains to this day (perhaps, in an Act of Penance, it's time the Bishop of St Davids moved back in). An English *Book of Common Prayer* is then foisted on a monoglot Welsh population with, predictably, little success, shoring up the popularity of the old Catholic rites.

Most people will not realise it, but Wales, like Ireland, remained stubbornly loyal to Mother Church long after England had succumbed, much to the frustration of English Puritan missionaries. It wasn't until the eighteenth century that the Protestant Reformation – in the sense of a genuine popular attachment and the full rejection of what later came to be known disdainfully as the Marian cult – could be said to have been completed in Wales, and only then because of a Third Wave of ecclesiastical colonisation that drafted anglophone Anglican priests in their hundreds into Welsh parishes and drove their long-suffering laity into the enthusiastic arms of the Methodist revivalists.

The Welsh, therefore – despite inhabiting the only part of the island of Britain with an unbroken Christian tradition – must join a long list of colonised peoples forced to change their religion as a consequence of conquest. Not content to steal our land, they then conspired to steal our souls. No wonder the poet Thomas ab Ieuan Rhys would lament, "We have been changed by the faith of the Saxons. Our hearts are not inclined towards it". Siôn Brwynog would speak in 1550 of the "icy coldness" of the new faith and the "bitter blow" of witnessing the removal of the altars and adjuncts of Catholic worship. Little wonder that when Guido Fawkes went to see Philip of Spain in 1603 – introduced most probably through the auspices of Hugh Owen of Plas Du, Hispanophile and the Continent's leading Catholic spy – to petition him in favour of an invasion, it was Milford Haven he proposed as the landing site, since Wales would prove the most fertile recruiting ground for a Catholic army.

A change of strategy, not a change in purpose, won Wales to the Protestant faith. Elizabethan state sponsorship of the translation of the Bible and the *Book of Common Prayer* should not be mistaken as an altogether altruistic measure. The final clause of the Act for the Translation of the Bible and Divine Service into the Welsh Tongue required an English Bible to be placed in every Welsh church so that the monoglot Welsh "may by conferring both Tongues together, the sooner attain to the knowledge of the English Tongue". Whatever William Morgan's motivation, the ultimate aim was the same as the Acts of Union themselves: anglicisation and uniformity. The fact that it had the opposite effect was more by accident than design.

The wider attack on the Welsh language probably represents the longest state-sanctioned policy of attempted linguistic genocide in history. A charter granted to Welshpool in 1406 stated that legal cases could only be pleaded henceforth in French or English. Six hundred years later, we are still pleading for Welsh to achieve equal status in the courts. The Acts of Union, with their condemnation of "sinister usages and customs", in Gwyn Alf Williams' words, rendered a "largely monoglot people aliens in their own land". With friends like the Tudors, who needed enemies.

The Victorians – for all their Celtomania – were determined to finish the job: even the arch-Celticist Matthew Arnold was to declare, "the sooner the Welsh language disappears as an instrument of the practical, political, social life of Wales, the better". With Arnold a senior inspector of schools, it hardly came as any surprise that the 1870 Education Act made English compulsory. It was to take until 1939 for the first Welsh-medium school to open – here in Aberystwyth. By then the damage had been done.

The most telling symbol of all of cultural imperialism in Wales, of course, was a little wooden tablet with the letters 'WN' branded into it that hung around the necks of children. The language was literally beaten out of us. But children were forced not just to betray their culture but also their classmates: the ultimate mental cruelty. The Welsh Not was the model for the corporal punishment of indigenous culture throughout the Empire; as a child, the Kenyan novelist Ngũgĩ wa Thiong'o wore a wooden tablet around his own neck which they called 'Monitor'. Any child speaking KiSwahili or Gikuyu would be given the Monitor until they heard another child do the same, so they could point them out to the teacher. The child left holding the Monitor at the end of the day would be beaten with a stick. Sound familiar?

That we were a subject people in political terms is also an objective fact, however uncomfortable we may be with its consequences. Wales, unlike the Scots or Irish Parliaments, was not consulted on its own Act of Union. We were to be rendered politically invisible, as things turned out, until the final year of the final century of the last Millennium. Our royal house was not conjoined through dynastic marriage; it was murdered. The heir to the English throne, a constituent of mine who admittedly has shown more genuine interest in Wales than all his predecessors put together, has about as much moral right to the title 'Prince of Wales' as Perkin Warbeck did to the English throne in the time of Henry VII. And it wasn't just descendants of Hywel Dda that were 'disappeared' like the victims of a military junta; his laws too were consigned to the garbage heap of history. Monmouthshire found itself lumped in with England for no better reason than the English circuits were composed of four counties – and Wales had thirteen, so Monmouthshire was forced to make up the numbers with its three English neighbours. That said, in the remaining twelve counties, the native law of Wales survived two of the three attempts to render them null and void. The Statute of Rhuddlan in the Welsh circuit courts soon evolved into the Statute of Wales, and a separate Welsh judicature developed which again somehow survived the Act of Union's legal lynching. Welsh law obviously embodied the spirit of Gwilym Crach of Gower, who was hung not once, but twice for his involvement in a rebellion of 1298, and still survived... The devil simply wouldn't die. So it was that even as late as 1779, Welsh defendants were employing the legal argument *"breve regis non currit in Walliam"* – the king's writ doesn't run in Wales. It wasn't until 1830, when the last great imperialist monarch Queen Victoria was just eleven years old, that the Welsh Court of Great Sessions was abolished, finally laying the legal legacy of Welsh independence to rest. At least until now.

The reasons for the colonisation of medieval Wales were probably more strategic than economic. Upland Wales helped supply England with beef, milk and wool, but its function as a buffer against foreign invasion was probably the main attraction. In the third wave of colonisation fuelled by the Industrial Revolution, that position was dramatically reversed when Wales became one of the most industrialised regions on the planet.

As Professor Merfyn Jones has said, Wales from 1850 can be caricatured as one big mine or quarry as some mineral or ore was being extracted virtually everywhere. Iron ore was dug and smelted here continuously from the late 1780s; at the same time Anglesey had a virtual world monopoly on copper and here in Ceredigion the mines were for lead and zinc. And yes, Wales was the only the part of modern Britain ever to see a gold rush, in Dolgellau in the 1880s.

Then there were all the different types of stone quarried here: limestone for the foundries, sandstone, dolerite, granite and, of course, slate, where north Wales represented the world's biggest producer for all of the nineteenth century and much of the twentieth. And I haven't even mentioned coal. By 1913, 35% of the tonnage of all Britain's exports was leaving through south Wales ports: almost all of it coal to fuel the industries and shipping of the world.

One of the most striking features of this impressive economic record is that it was led, with a very few exceptions, by English proprietors. The Cyfarthfa Iron Works, for example, which turned Merthyr into an economic powerhouse, was founded by Anthony Bacon from Cumbria. He was followed by the Crawshays from Yorkshire and the Guests of Shropshire. The

Ebbw Vale Iron Works was established by the Homfrays of Staffordshire. In north Wales, it was John Wilkinson of Cumbria who led the way. The metal industry in Swansea, meanwhile, was developed by the Vivian family from Cornwall.

There were some exceptions – the copper and coal kings Thomas Williams and David Davies, for example – but on the whole the pattern was clear. John Taylor, the leading figure in the Welsh lead industry, was from Norwich. A new class of alien or absentee landowners were also at the forefront of development. The Grosvenor family, ancestors of the current Duke of Westminster, was involved in lead mining in north-east Wales. A Cheshire family, the Assheton Smiths of the Faenol Estate, made their fortune in slate. The Butes made vast profits not only from coal but from the ports they built to export it. Even in agriculture, the almost feudal level of absentee ownership persisted late into the nineteenth century. In 1887 less than 5% of the land in Caernarfonshire was owned by its tenants.

With such a high level of English ownership, we bore all of the human and environmental cost but saw little of the profit – with the exception of a few square miles of civic pride in Cardiff. Instead follies and mock-feudal mansions were built the length and breadth of Wales. This was the Welsh equivalent of what economists call the 'resource curse': the fact that mineral wealth is almost always more trouble than it's worth. The 'path dependence' created by an extractive mono-culture is still with us today: our failure to develop an indigenous enterprise culture and, as George Monbiot has recently pointed out, the preponderance of east-west over north-south links, both stem from the colonial exploitation of our economy.

Beyond economic domination and military conquest, as the late Edward Said was able to show, colonialism is also, of course, a discourse of domination: a deep-seated idea that the imperial power has an inherent right to rule and impose its values on the nation that it dominates. So it was that the

Anglo-Norman propagandists opened up a 'cultural front' in their war against the Welsh which has formed the bedrock to Cambrophobia down the centuries.

So it is that the author of the twelfth-century English history *The Deeds of King Stephen* informs us: "Wales is a country of wooded pasture that breeds men of an animal type, swift-footed, accustomed to war, volatile, quick in breaking their word and changing their abode", omitting to mention that the Welsh also lived in towns until the Normans drove them out, and that the need to fight and keep constantly on the move may have had something to do with his kinsmen's presence.

When Chrétien De Troyes says, in writing *Peredur* or *Perceval* – one of a number of Welsh characters to populate the European romantic imagination for the best part of a millennium, not bad for a people 'on the edge' – "All Welshmen are, by nature, more irrational than animals in the field", he is not just echoing the views of the Anglo-Norman elite, but also presaging the classic strategy of rendering the colonised as the savage 'Other' used centuries later by European powers in Africa, Asia or America. He also represents a tradition that continues right through to the nineteenth-century view of portraying the Celtic personality as irrational, childlike, impractical and racially inferior.

A second recurring theme is that of our immorality. The Normans justify their takeover of the Welsh Church by reference to the loose morals of their flock, who practised trial marriage, homosexuality, and inheritance rights for the illegitimate. We were, it seems, prodigiously modern. It is here that the continuity of colonialism re-emerges. When the infamous *Report of the Commissioners of Inquiry into the state of Education in Wales* of 1847 ('The Treachery of the Blue Books') was published, it was again the moral laxity of the Welsh that was held up as the most pressing reason for making English the sole medium of instruction.

In those periods where the Welsh demonstrate passivity and obedience then a different picture of the Welsh is presented:

as comically stupid, if a little two-faced. In the eighteenth and nineteenth centuries there was a rich market for this kind of thing: Taffy and his wife sat atop a goat – because they couldn't afford a horse – leeks poking out of their hats, holding a cheese in one hand and their pedigree in the other.

There was often a modern sinister undertow. In 1885 John Beddoe, President of the Anthropological Institute, had developed an Index of Nigrescence which claimed to show that the Welsh and western Irish were 'Africanoid' in their 'jutting jaws' and 'slitty nostrils' and thus originally immigrants from Africa. This idea of the Celts as 'colonials' had been a constant theme since the Age of Discovery: as one Protestant pamphleteer said in 1651, frustrated at the lack of success in converting the Welsh, "We have Indians at home – Indians in Cornwall, Indians in Wales, Indians in Ireland." Forget sending missionaries to the West Indies, he argued, send them to Carmarthenshire.

So it is that the prevailing image of the Welsh in England throughout these three colonial periods ranges from submissive and deferential to lewd and unruly, and even downright perfidious, on a par with that of the wild Irish. What never changed was the tacit assumption that we were by definition inferior.

The lowest point was the passing of the Punitive Laws in the wake of the Glyndŵr Rebellion, which introduced a system of racial discrimination equal to apartheid. These race laws have fallen prey to a collective amnesia so it is worth recounting them in full: from 1401, no Welshman was to enjoy the privilege of burgess status (an absolute prohibition traditionally reserved for the Jews); no Welshman was to buy land in England; no Welshman was to hold a major office in Wales. These prohibitions extended to any Englishman who had married a Welsh woman since the revolt began. No Welshman was to carry arms in any town, market, church assembly or highway. No Welshman was to hold a castle or any other defensible house that had existed in the time of Edward I. Garrisons would comprise exclusively of Englishmen – not even men of mixed nationality would be allowed. No Englishman was to be convicted in Wales by, or at the suit of, a Welshman.

As R R Davies argued, what is particularly striking about these edicts is that they are "specifically racist in character". An extreme reaction to the shock of the Glyndŵr revolt they undoubtedly were – but they were also reinstating the common-law practice of three hundred years of English supremacism. Kidwelly, created in the 1100s, had English, French and Flemish burgesses – but no Welsh (or *forinseci*). We were literally foreigners in our own land. In 1351 the ironically named Hope in Flintshire banned the Welsh from holding burgages and confiscated any that already did – but this was nothing new: Edward I had banned Welshmen from holding land or bearing arms in borough towns in reaction to Madog ap Llywelyn's revolt of 1294.

The attitudes that underpinned the Punitive Laws have re-emerged at other times in our colonial past, and overt discrimination continued to be part of our experience in Wales right through into the modern period.

For the first part of the eighteenth century, for example, the majority of the Welsh, by virtue of their Nonconformity, were banned from taking office in the House of Commons. For the same reason, they couldn't enter Oxford or Cambridge until 1871 – this being one of the principal drivers behind the establishment of the University of Wales.

We were a colony. And now we're in a state of denial. The factual evidence for the reality of colonisation is all around us – indeed it can even be said to be within us. But to the extent that we acknowledge it, it might as well be invisible. Dilys Davies, a Welsh psychiatrist working at Guy's Hospital who has conducted an exhaustive analysis of the Welsh psyche, has called this a form of cultural autism and drawn analogies with child sexual abuse, which for all its pervasiveness was once met by a wall of silence. Colonisation is our 'dangerous idea', a 'dirty little secret', a 'painful memory' that has to be repressed. Cambridge University Press' primer on Medieval Wales warns the reader that in Wales' case "the colonial analogy – may be pushed too far and it must be used with great sensitivity". The late, great R R Davies – whose revolutionary tracts 'Colonial Wales' and 'Race Relations in Post-Conquest Wales' were published within a year of each other in the mid 1970s as he moved to Aberystwyth – was very much the glorious exception. He himself was warned that specialising in Welsh history was reputational suicide for a young Welsh historian and, sadly, he never got to teach a course on the history of his own country here at Aberystwyth, though he is one of the greatest historians that Wales has produced.

So it was left to Gwynfor Evans to continue where the professional historians left off. When Michael Hechter produced his magnum opus, *Internal Colonialism: The Celtic Fringe in British National Development*, he was met with a chorus of disapproval from Welsh academics. Alfred Zimmern could have warned him, perhaps, of the professional perils of an outsider prognosticating about issues of Welsh identity.

In some ways, the robust rejection of the theory of 'internal colonialism' was in part a reaction to myths perpetrated by colonialism itself – that Wales was a backwater, outside the mainstream of modernity, and the Welsh a people whose history was lived perpetually in the passive tense. For Gwyn Alf Williams, Wales' global industrial pre-eminence meant the Welsh Working Class – always capitalised – were "junior partners in the British Empire". Casting back to Tudor times, he showed how that latter-day Merlin, Dr John Dee, used the Madoc myth to stake a British claim to the New World – British, if you please, the Welsh at the Tudor Court having reconquered Albion for the Celts. Far from being victims of the British Empire, in this version of history, we invented it.

There can certainly be no doubt that the Welsh enthusiastically embraced imperialism. Though less prominent than the Scots, the Welsh were well represented among the military and civilian ranks of Imperial Britain. At one time, the Chief Justices of both Bengal and Calcutta were Welsh-speaking Welshmen. But does the sight of Zulu spearing Welshmen at the Battle of Isandlwhana, or Welshmen bayoneting Zulu at the Battle of Rorke's Drift in return, help or hinder the hypothesis that Britishness was forged by all four nations of these islands in the cauldron of empire which became the Britannic melting-pot, as Gordon Brown's favourite historian, Linda Colley, suggests? Could this not simply be a rather poignant reminder of the practice of empires since time immemorial of pressing the already-vanquished into doing the next bit of vanquishing?

Of course we participated in later imperial adventures. Denied opportunities for advancement at home, we often had little choice. But this obscures the bigger truth, that where other colonies were the copy, we were the original, where colonialism's die was first minted. It was the Marcher Lords, like the de Lacys who founded Drogheda, who sought in the first instance to pacify Ireland, able to draw as they were on a century or more of experience of colonial occupation in Wales. The peopling of Pembrokeshire by Flemings presaged the later Plantation of Ulster. The Tudors held up post-conquest Wales as the model for recalcitrant Ireland. As Sir Henry Sidney's secretary William Gerard assured the Privy Council on the occasion of his master's transfer from Wales to Ireland, "A better president [precedent].....colde not be founde than to imitate the course that reformed Wales."

Wales was the epicentre for three tidal waves of colonial expansion in the history of the Anglo-British state: the insular colonialism of the Norman period, the transatlantic ambitions of the Tudors and the global imperialism of the Victorians. We supplied the model for the first, the myth for the second and the material for the third. In each phase, we paid a heavy price for our collusion in our own enslavement with the progressive colonisation of our own minds and imaginations. The first English imperialists were early amateurs at this kind of thing – but come the Treason of the Blue Books, they had learned to deploy it to devastating effect.

Colonialism in any society and in any period is an act of violation which results in trauma whose effects are felt for many generations. Hence the most long-lasting and deep-seated legacy of colonialism is psychological. It was the mixed-race French-speaking Caribbean Frantz Fanon, practising psychiatry and preaching revolution in occupied Algeria, who first realised this and began to write painfully but eloquently about the psychology of colonialism. Welsh psychologists and psychotherapists by contrast have been almost completely silent on this theme. Dr Dilys Davies of Guy's Hospital, the only professional psychiatrist to have written at all about colonialism's effect on the Welsh psyche, suggests that – as with R R Davies the historian – it is not in the professional interests of the Welsh psychiatrist to appear too 'parochial'. Dr Davies, by contrast, stands out as the Frantz Fanon of Wales and virtually the entirety of what follows is based on her pioneering work.

As with many other things, the Irish have a head start on us in thinking about the psychology of colonialism. An important feature, according to the psychologist Vincent Kenny, is the way in which the Irish have internalised their own oppression. One way of overcoming the feeling of powerlessness that flows from being dominated is to identify with the dominator – sometimes even unconsciously. It is a kind of sociological equivalent of Stockholm syndrome – what Fanon calls "adhesion" to the dominator, the Brazilian pedagogist Paulo Freire called "housing the other" and the German-Jewish psychologist Erich Fromm called an "inner duality". It goes by many names, but its self-destructive consequences are all too obvious: our selves become divided against ourselves. We become self-oppressing. It should be no surprise, therefore, that Beriah Gwynfe Evans, the Secretary of Cymru Fydd, was an enthusiastic exponent of the Welsh Not as a young teacher – and that its use was far more widespread among voluntary schools prior to 1870 than in state schools thereafter, implying that parents generally approved of its use. 'Was Welsh as the language of the majority murdered or did it commit suicide?' is the question often posed. The question is in some ways irrelevant because both realities are in fact the parallel outcomes of the selfsame process (the Welsh Not was also an early example of the invidious effects of performance-related pay – since the teachers were paid by results and Welsh didn't form part of the formal curriculum, the use of Welsh was actively discouraged by the teachers).

That we have been complicit in our own colonisation is undeniable. As Gandhi said of his own country: "The English have not taken India; we have given it to them." In developing this theme in his *Hind Swaraj* ('Indian Home Rule'), Gandhi drew upon a little-known treatise by an 18-year-old Frenchman, Étienne de la Boétie, written some 15 years after our own Act of Union: the 'Discourse on Voluntary Servitude'. In it he argues that structures of power in any situation, even where they rely on physical force, depend in the last analysis on the consent – however reluctant – of those over whom power is exercised. As Gandhi went on to say: "It is we the English-knowing Indians that have enslaved India. The curse of the nation will rest not upon the English but upon us..."

So how has colonialism's curse imprinted itself on the modern Welsh psyche? Broadly speaking, the effects can be divided into two categories: the way in which we see ourselves, and the way in which we interact with others.

The former flows from the central fact of domination itself. Conquered peoples are often perceived as passive, a little fatalistic, prone to introspection. The writer René Marqués has written, for example, about the docile nature of his compatriot Puerto Ricans. And how much has been written about the melancholia of the Celts? But as Erich Fromm pointed out, rather than this being an essential part of our national character from the start, it simply reflects our actual historic experience of being downtrodden. So Welsh music is sung in the minor key, and our poetry adopts an elegaic tone. In political terms, we develop a begging bowl mentality because have become resigned to the reality of our own domination. We feel a sense of helplessness and hopelessness – what J J Lee has called, in the Irish case, the "peasant residue" in our psyche. We abdicate responsibility for our own future because we doubt our ability to act constructively and change our situation. We avoid taking risks and prefer security, even if that means locking ourselves into relative poverty and unrealised potential. Above all, we suffer from a profound sense of our own inferiority, a lack of confidence which expresses itself through our failure to show initiative, whether in political or business terms.

It is this deep insecurity that I believe lies at the heart of our still-tentative embrace of devolution, and our rejection of what is, after all, the normal aspiration of any nation: political independence. It also, in the economic sphere, explains our overweening reliance on public subsidy and our failure so far to develop, in sufficient numbers at least, an indigenous entrepreneurial class. We are economically dependent because we are psychologically dependent, and vice versa. And we reject political independence because of both.

Colonialism casts an equally insidious shadow on the way in which we communicate and relate to each other. We are a nation of indirect communicators, frightened to criticise in case we upset 'the powers that be' and lose face, or even worse, are punished financially. We are unwilling to be 'pinned down' and fearful of being 'put down'. The number of Welsh social scientists, for example, that are prepared to make statements that could be seen as controversial can be counted on the fingers of one hand. The number of Welsh MPs who have criticised the Welsh National Opera and the British Lions is limited to one. For a country with a rich Nonconformist,

45

anti-Establishment tradition, we are – in our own context – incredibly conformist and establishmentarian. This is a typical survival tactic for a conquered people, where direct challenges to authority are to be avoided at all cost. Instead we learn to be evasive, complaining to each other about someone else instead of tackling the person directly. This is how we earned our reputation for being devious and two-faced. We had to be.

But it also feeds into aspects of community life, especially in Welsh-speaking Wales, where a taboo against self-promotion or self-revelation, a tendency for self-censorship and deference to authority among local people contrasts with the assertiveness of the in-migrant population. Native Welsh speakers are often the majority in public meetings but will often remain stoically silent – even where translation facilities are available – and let others 'dominate' the meeting.

This self-censorship in the public realm is perhaps the flipside of another aspect of Welsh cultural psychology: a withdrawal to an inner world of self-reflection: "the everlasting Welsh habit has been to sink inwards", according to John Cowper Powys. But how does this fit with the Welsh love of performance on the stage or the playing field, where we suddenly shape-shift from a nation of passive spectators to a nation of exhibitionists? The answer can be found in the 'theory of constriction' developed by the American George Kelly in the 1950s, whereby the realms in which we can 'be ourselves' are socially controlled. So it was that the Welsh language came to be limited to the emotive worlds of the sacred, the lyrical and the familial, and progressively banished from the world of the secular, official or practical.

These psychological manifestations of colonialism are not accidental by-products of broad historical processes. They are the outcome of two quite deliberate strategies of cultural alienation. The first one can be termed manipulation; inculcating within the mind of the dominated the dominator's myths, their version of reality, their language, their values. So

Paulo Freire argues that at a crucial juncture in their existential development, members of the dominated group begin to aspire to the same way of life as the dominator. So they start to imitate them, follow them and talk like them. When Chrétien de Troyes' Peredur first sets out for Court, his mother persuades him to leave two of his three javelins at home, "because they look too Welsh". We have been leaving our javelins at home ever since. (Of course, this comes at a cost. As Aneurin Bevan quipped, when someone accused Roy Jenkins of lacking application, no-one who came from Abersychan and spoke like that could ever be accused of laziness.) So we have a succession of groups that anglicise themselves in order to improve their life chances: starting with the *uchelwyr* ('nobility') who become the Welsh gentry and eventually the hated absentee landlords of the eighteenth century. But this percolated right the way down the social strata: the Welsh language came to be seen as 'a badge of poverty'. Working-class parents – like my own – decided consciously not to pass it on to their children, in order to improve their children's chances in life.

The third wave of Welsh colonisation, thus, was not conducted by military means. There was no need, as John Davies reminds us, quoting the author of a nineteenth-century 'Report on the Condition of the South Wales Coalfield': "a band of efficient schoolmasters is kept up at much less expense than a body of police or soldiery." Our enslavement was sold back to us as the means to our own liberation. So the 1870 Education Act, actually marking the beginning of the decline of Welsh as a national language, was presented as a victory for the Welsh ideal of universal education. The 1536 Act of Union was dressed up as being about equal rights for Welsh and English subjects, and the restoration of the rightful Brythonic claim to the throne. Even Henry VII appropriated Arthurian myth to bolster his imperial ambitions – naming his firstborn after the most famous of all our messianic figures. Come the Reformation, the Anglican Church presented itself as a recreation of the Celtic

Church, freed from the Romanising influences of Catholicism. Jesus College, Oxford – deliberately designed as a tool in the indoctrination of the sons of the Welsh elite – was presented as an act of munificence on the part of Good Queen Bess.

The second generic cultural strategy of the dominator is summed up by the famous formula: divide and rule. The more a community can be broken up into separate parts, the less their sense of belonging to their own community, the easier it is to maintain dominance. This strategy was used by the British to devastating effect through the caste system in India and tribal divisions in Africa – divisions which have persisted long after independence. The Normans set about dividing Wales into two opposing camps of urban English settlement and rural Welsh. We have seen ourselves ever since as a country of two peoples, two cultures, divided between the city and the country, north and south, English-speaking and Welsh speaking – our divisions magnified and distorted deliberately to play one group off against each other. So it was during the devolution campaign of 1979 that No leaflets in north Wales would say that the Assembly would be dominated by the urban, more populous English-speaking south, whereas No leaflets in the south – you guessed it – warned of an Assembly dominated by Welsh-speaking farmers from Gwynedd.

So if you want to understand Welsh politics today, look to its roots: historical and psychological. We are in a country that has been in an almost-permanent state of existential crisis. We voted ourselves out of existence in 1979, came close to doing it a second time in 1997, and are now worried that we might do it again. Our physical proximity to and economic reliance on the colonial power has crushed our autonomy and made us dependent. In fact, it has infantilized us. The arrangements of the Government of Wales Act 2006 – whereby requests for power are scrutinised in London and may be refused – is totemic of an attitude that regards the Welsh polity, and by extension the Welsh people, as too immature to make their own laws.

The forthcoming referendum [the March 2011 referendum on legislative powers for the Welsh Assembly] is more than just a referendum on our system of government; it is a referendum on our state of mind as a nation, our dignity and our self-respect. It is an opportunity for us as a nation to start to draw a line under our experience of colonialism. As it will be the first referendum that we ourselves have initiated, it will be the first direct expression of our own sovereignty and our right to equality in these islands.

Since colonialism, as the Indian theorist Ashis Nandy tells us, is first of all a matter of consciousness, it has to be defeated at the level of the human imagination. Politics alone will not succeed. This struggle must be waged as a battle of ideas, new cultural practices and economic behaviours. In a sense, outside of the language struggle, our nationalism has been too much focused on nation-building as a process of creating representative institutions rather than thinking about the Wales we want those institutions to represent. There is an echo here of Saunders Lewis' parting shot in his history-shaping lecture *Tynged yr Iaith* ('The Fate of the Language'), where he warns that the decline of the language might actually be accelerated unless we undergo the cultural change in mindset needed before independence itself is achieved. The Irish experience is clearly implied. The failure of Ireland on bilingualism – and on the economy until the 1980s – points to a much deeper truth: that formal independence is meaningless unless we have first decolonised our minds. As Irish historian J J Lee has written:

> The incapacity of the Irish mind to think through the implications of independence for national development derived largely from, and was itself a symbol of, the dependency syndrome which had wormed its way into the Irish psyche during the centuries of foreign dominance.

The first step in national liberation is mental. Cultural revitalisation always predates political renewal, just as Dafydd ap Gwilym predated Owain Glyndŵr. As nationalists, the lesson is clear: we should each of us start to think and behave prefiguratively, as if our nation is already free. We must be the Wales we want to create: a vibrant, self-empowering, dynamic country that emphasises the power of our own initiative.

Of course, we can never escape from our colonial past by refusing to acknowledge it. To liberate ourselves, we have to learn about ourselves. On the psychology of colonialism itself, we need more research. We need to move from a culture of silence to a culture of salience. There is an *Irish Journal of Psychology* and an *Australian Journal of Psychology*. A *Welsh Journal of Psychology* is long overdue, and a Welsh Institute of Psychiatry would be a good idea too. More generally, we have to detach ourselves from the insular intellectual straitjacket in which we find ourselves – in which Welsh literature, Welsh psychology, Welsh history and Welsh politics are still seen as subaltern specialisms in more mainstream disciplines.

To bypass the dyad of domination between ourselves and the former imperial capital, Wales must find a new context as a European nation, in the same way that Llywelyn and Glyndŵr sought allies in France. Europeanising Wales means that our experience of domination can be understood as by no means exceptional nor ineluctably permanent. Building on the success of the last fifty years of bilingual education, now is the time to campaign for tri-lingual schools, immersing students from Welsh-speaking homes in French, German or Russian just as effectively as English-speaking children in Welsh. We have long claimed a greater facility in other languages as one of the advantages of being bilingual. It's time to prove it.

In education more broadly, we need what Paulo Freire originally called "a pedagogy of the oppressed". Developing Welsh as a medium of instruction was the first vital step; gaining control of the content of the curriculum the next. But the third vital ingredient – transforming the very nature of the teaching process itself – we are only now beginning to embark upon. But it is here where the truly revolutionary potential of teaching lies. Education in Wales – informed by a conservative grammarial tradition, and historically taught in people's second language, where education was seen primarily not as a route to knowledge, even less self-knowledge, but, for the lucky few at least, the route out of poverty and all too often the route out of Wales – has also been a domain of prescription rather than development. As Dilys Davies has said:

> Education with the ideological intent… of unquestioning adoption resists dialogue and critical thought and treats its students as objects. The students are not called upon to know but to memorize the contents narrated by the teacher.

When Welsh was finally appended to the curriculum, this 'mechanical drilling' of learning-by-rote was then later applied with disastrous ineffectiveness to the teaching of Welsh as a second language to those that had lost it.

In the new Foundation Phase we have the chance of a new start for a new generation. In ditching formal teaching for three to seven year olds and adopting, on the Finnish model, a strategy of learning through play, we have finally broken with the regimented learning of 1870 on. And when I say regimented, I choose my words advisedly. The model of formal learning adopted with the advent of compulsory schooling in Britain was the same one that spread throughout Europe following the Prussian policy of compulsory education, which was first developed in response to their defeat at the hands of Napoleon at the Battle of Jena. Schools were to become factories which would turn out obedient soldiers for the army, subservient workers for the mines and submissive civil servants for government. Independent thought – and in our case, an independent language – was to be beaten out of our children. We have finally begun to lay this ghost to rest.

With this new emphasis on developing our innate creativity, we have the potential to become a nation of entrepreneurs, both individual and collective. Our only sure means of finally putting paid to the dependency myth is to show, by example, that we can be economically successful – in business, and also by developing business models that chime more readily with our own collaborative and egalitarian system of values than the rapacious Anglo-American ideal of heroic individualism. The *Dictionary of Welsh Biography* of the twenty-first century should be as defined by innovators of every description as the nineteenth-century version was peopled by ministers of religion. One important contribution might be to create an English-language version of Menter a Busnes – which has been using a range of techniques to promote enterprise culture among Welsh speakers for two decades, with increasing signs of success.

A final imperative has to be the creation of a new unified pan-Wales sense of identity. This undoubtedly is the biggest failure of the national movement. The language movement did manage, in the words of a young Cynog Dafis, "to effect some kind of transformation in the Welsh psychology". But the counter-colonial counter-culture it helped foster has largely been self-contained within the Welsh-speaking community. Reaching out to English-language Wales is partly a political task: the most socially disadvantaged in Wales today – in Hechter's terms, the modern equivalents of "hewers of wood and drawers of water" – unskilled English-speaking women, is the category that is least likely to vote Plaid. We cannot truly claim to be a national party until we change that.

But at the level of the country as a whole, we need to turn nation-building into a personal experience. We could usefully learn from the Canadian experiment of *Katimavik* in the 1980s, a voluntary twelve-month national civilian service programme whereby young people got to spend time working with other young Canadians in the different provinces of Canada. Huw Lewis has recently suggested immersing Welsh learners in the Welsh-language culture by billeting them with families in the West. I agree, but let's do it in reverse too and have young Welsh women and men from the north and the west spending time in the Valleys and our cities.

If we do all this, then unlike Ireland in 1921, when independence finally comes – as come it will – we will have a generation that has been prepared for it.

Will we be the final colony? Well, that of course is up to us. In the words of Antonio Machado:

> our footprints are the only road;
> nothing else;
> we make the road as we travel

Somebody said to me recently that Welsh independence is a bit like nuclear fusion: it is always a generation away. But in a sense it has been ever thus. I am personally hopeful. If Siôn Cent, warming himself with the dying embers of Glyndŵr's memory and what might have been, could still say, 'My Hope Is On What Is To Come', then I too can find reasons to be an optimist.

Wales was not just colonised, but re-colonised and then, for good measure, re-colonised again. We somehow survived Norman *blitzkreig*, Tudor *lebensraum* and Victorian eugenics. We have survived for a reason. And the reason lies within us; buried, however deep within.

4

We are the ones we have been waiting for

A chapter from *25/25 Vision: Welsh horizons across 50 years*, published in 2012 to mark the 25th anniversary of the Institute of Welsh Affairs

FROM BERLIN TO the Baltic States, 1989 was a time of revolution. To my mind, this is the year that Wales too came in from the cold. I was studying in Germany when the Wall came down. I saw tears in my German friends' eyes as the news came in, drinking with them till the early hours as they hugged, in a state of incomprehension at the utter magnitude of it all.

1989 was a hinge-point in our history too, though by now one that's almost forgotten. The Pontypridd by-election, following the death from exhaustion of Brynmor John, was held on 23 February that year. The poll was called unseasonably early, presumably to prevent Welsh Nationalism building up the same terrifying momentum that the SNP had displayed a few months earlier at Jim Sillars' great triumph in Govan. In the cold of a Valleys winter, this was to be no Spring Awakening. Change was in the air, but then so was the snow.

I shivered from daybreak to dusk. Sleeping on the floor with a Plaid family, I'd somehow become separated from my coat. Voters watched as words dripped like stalactites from my breath. A teenage friend from Richmond, Simon Brooks, a fellow Marxist and Welsh learner who went on to edit the magazine *Barn* ('Opinion') and found community pressure group Cymuned, lent me his jacket in a spirit of solidarity. We felt but didn't fear the cold, imbued with that strange passionate intensity you know when you are young and writing history. That didn't stop me being told off by the Plaid Women's Section when Simon was found hypothermic outside a polling station somewhere near Church Village.

Kim Howells, the Labour candidate, had warned of the danger posed by "students from Aberystwyth" being bussed in in their hundreds, making us sound like some People's Liberation Army on manoeuvres – though the Provisional wing of the Urdd would probably be more apt. There were sons of the Manse from the north here experiencing real Valleys life for the very first time. For us young partisans, canvassing was nation-building, one street at a time.

For me, this election was infused with a totemic significance. The NUM had shaped my politics every bit as much as it had for Kim. The annual Miners' Gala was where I heard my first political speeches, and where I bought my first political book (heavily subsidised, courtesy of Moscow). Though it was to Dafydd El's party that my family defected in the wake of Kinnock's great betrayal, Kim remained something of a hero, an archetypal Valleys intellectual, proletarian and urbane. A passionate advocate for the Wales Congress – the National Assembly in embryo – he was, like its founder and fellow historian, Hywel Francis, a card-carrying Communist, hence gratifyingly liberated from the granite-like grip of Labour's stifling hegemony.

I cannot even now quite express the depth of my shock and disappointment at Kim's swift descent from working-class hero to career politician, plucked straight from the pages of *Fame is the Spur*. It was as if Gareth Edwards had 'gone north' after 'that try'. How had the leather-jacketed NUM official of *Ms Rhymney Valley 1984* morphed into this besuited Mandelson-approved mouthpiece for the rebranded Labour Party? The truth is, of course, that Kim was New Labour before New Labour even existed. Sharp as a miner's pick, he knew the British Labour Party needed to appeal beyond industrial workers in places like Pontypridd if it ever wanted to share the spoils of power again. It was a theme he'd first developed in John Osmond's 1988 documentary series *The Divided Kingdom*. The writing was on the colliery wall. Radical Wales had to be sacrificed on the altar of Middle England.

When Neil Kinnock described Plaid Cymru, in a missive to party activists at the beginning of the campaign, as a "puny force", he was exaggerating for effect. But at the preceding General Election the Party of Wales had indeed received just 5% of the vote, behind the Alliance candidate and even the hated Conservatives. Plaid had been in continuous electoral retreat since 1979, Gwyn Alf Williams' *'blwyddyn y pla'* ('year of plague'). Plaid's National Left had won every election internally – most notably the election of Dafydd Elis Thomas as President – but popular support had failed to materialise, Ieuan Wyn Jones' impressive victory in Anglesey in the 1987 general election notwithstanding.

By-elections in some ways are the lightning conductors of political history – and this was the election that had inscribed within it the arc of our times. On the cusp of the campaign, sensing perhaps the improbable resurgence of Welsh nationalism – a creed he disdained like no other – Kinnock, the anti-hero of 1979, now suddenly declared a conversion to the cause of devolution every bit as sudden as Saul of Tarsus' transformation into Saint Paul.

Only a week or so earlier he had talked about splitting Wales possibly into three 'administrative divisions', a Napoleonic proposal which the Chair of the Wales Labour Executive was forced to admit lacked the support of a single respondent to the Party's own devolution consultation. Plaid's Syd Morgan was instantly installed in pole position as challenger ahead of a youthful Nigel Evans for the Tories – and soon Neil Kinnock was announcing he had finally come off the fence (was he ever on it?) on the side of a democratically elected Welsh Senate, Plaid's tentative proposal just two years earlier. His deputy, hoary old radical Roy Hattersley, even went as far as calling for a law-making and fully tax-raising Assembly, way ahead of official policy even 23 years later. Nevertheless, the logjam of Labour's opposition to Welsh self-government had, at long last, been removed.

In the event, Plaid's support surged by 20%, the best nationalist result in a by-election since Emrys Roberts' near-miss in Merthyr in 1972. I joined the dreaded Aber students in booing the newly-elected Labour MP for Pontypridd, earning the disapproval of the leader writer of the *South Wales Echo*.

I was, as it happens, to see Kim a number of times over the years. The next time was at a party thrown by my first employer, another remarkable product of the grammar schools of the Cynon Valley, Kevin Morgan – a Cardiff academic recently returned from Brighton, who was later to lead the1997 Yes Campaign to victory. I told Kim, with all the precocious authority a young researcher could muster, "I'll see you in the House." I did, but we hardly spoke. We had, by then, little to say to each other.

Kevin and I first met because of my own first faltering attempts to get elected. I lost the Presidency of NUS Wales, which Plaid had held since a certain Alun Davies had stormed the barricades, by just one vote. Tony Benn – another of my political heroes – had even come down to the Aberavon Beach Hotel to expound on the iniquities of nationalism. Four weeks to go to finals and I was running out of heroes, and didn't have a job. But I'd heard about an exciting new research project involving Kevin and another of Wales' trinity of great innovation theorists, Phil Cooke (the third being their former student, now Professor Robert Huggins. If only we Welsh were as good at innovation practice as we are at theory, so the joke goes, we could be Singapore).

The project was a by-product of the Four Motors programme – an EU grouping of the four most dynamic regions in Germany, France, Italy and Spain – to which Wales had been granted 'observer status' in 1992. It all stemmed from the original agreement signed in March 1990 by Wyn Roberts and the magisterial Minister-President of Baden-Württemberg, Lothar Späth. It was this – not, as Rhodri Morgan later mused, the 2002 Memorandum of Understanding Jane Davidson agreed with Cuba – that represented the first piece of independent Welsh foreign policy since the Pennal Letter. As Minister of State, or *Staatsminister,* in the Welsh Office, Stuttgart assumed the Welshman Sir Wyn, not Peter Walker, to be the more senior Minister. A delicious irony which meant it was a Welsh Christian Democrat – Sir Wyn could hardly be described as a Conservative in the narrowly British sense – who was the first politician in history to be flanked by motorcycle outriders with a Welsh flag proudly emblazoned on the official limousine.

Each decade carries within it the seeds of the next and the scars of the last. The Yes vote of 1997 was as much a rejection of Thatcherism as an embrace of Welsh self-government. Perversely, however, it was also fuelled by the very success of those definitely Welsh institutions created or expanded by the Conservatives themselves – the pre-Redwood Welsh Office, the pre- and post-Gwyn Jones Welsh Development Agency, and the harbingers of the new language consensus, S4C and the Welsh Language Board. The Nineties was our Decade of Late Expectation. A nation – or at least its intelligentsia, its civil society and the more nationally-minded of its political class – which had for so long felt buffeted by the cruel winds of history, at long last felt that same wind in its wings. It was a time of plans and blueprints, a publishing energy every bit as electrifying as the age of the nineteenth-century pamphleteer. I spent most of the decade in Aberystwyth – a town which was to Welsh nationalism as Zürich was to the Bolsheviks: a great town of plotters, who would meet by day in the Cabin and by night in the Cŵps. It still is the spiritual capital of Wales to me, to which all roads lead and beyond which lies only the sea. It was there in the heart of Ceredigion that I toasted my native Carmarthenshire for giving us an Assembly in Cardiff, a panegyric to a pan-Welsh future. I would have kissed someone from north Wales, too, but they were probably all at the bar.

If revolutions devour their children, then devolution devoured its parents. That compelling critique of the Quango State was the death-warrant of the WDA, and, later, the Welsh Language Board. Gone too are the Training and Enterprise Councils; most of the Local Enterprise Agencies; the Development Board for Rural Wales; the Media Agency for Wales, *Sgrîn*; Education and Learning Wales (ELWa); and soon, perhaps, the University of Wales. Of all the major public institutions threatened with abolition, only the Arts Council has survived, behind the protective veil of a Royal Charter. It is a strange quirk of history that the land so besmirched by the Blue Books should now be so fond of Commissioners.

It was, of course, always one of the peculiar features of Welsh public life that we lacked the institutional richness of Scotland or pre-independence Ireland, with their separate legal jurisdictions, note-issuing banks, historic universities, discretely established Churches and flourishing national press. The oligarchy of the past has been removed, hallelujah, but we have been left with something no less troubling. Under devolution, the institutional topography of Wales has become depressingly flat.

The starkly centripetal forces at work in Welsh society mean radical dissent, in this nation of radical dissenters, is increasingly marginalised. Those few academics and others who are willing to challenge orthodoxy are soon sidelined and branded 'unreliable'. Contemporary Wales is thankfully a long way from Putin's Russia, but it is no gilded monument to Jeffersonian democracy either. The power of patronage in Wales is as strong now as it ever was, and the true public sphere, the agora of the mind, is correspondingly diminished. Once the world's most Nonconformist of nations, we have become the global capital of conformism.

I spent most of my most youth on the floor, being heckled by the platform – usually by Labour councillors twice my size and three times my age. I see little in the culture of Welsh politics, or the politics of Welsh culture, that has fundamentally changed. Welsh politics is still largely a series of power plays in one act for one actor. Coalitions are the intervals when Labour has to learn not a monologue, but to dance. When the music stops, the New Politics dies. In the creativity-crushing environment favoured by the permanent inhabitants of Tŷ Hywel's Fifth Floor, it should come as little surprise that only around 10%–20% of the Welsh population want Wales to become an independent country (depending on the question the pollsters ask). If independent thinking is vigorously suppressed, then so too is thinking about independence. What is more troubling is that the thumping 80%–90% thumbs-up for Wales' current subordinate status is such a massive source of pride to so many of our self-styled leaders. What other nation in history has wallowed so much in its own self-abnegation?

This could be dismissed as a spasm of regret from a member of a frustrated minority. But the reality is that our rejection of responsibility for our own fate has at its root the same debilitating self-doubt that blights all aspects of our national life. This poverty of aspiration is to be seen everywhere, from our health statistics to our economy. It is to be seen on the faces of those that Wales has left behind – the higher numbers of NEETs (Not in Education, Employment or Training) in Wales now than before devolution who feel, with hearts accepting darkness, that there is no better option, no better way.

For them the era of devolution, far from offering some economic dividend, has crushed their hope like the coal in their grandfathers' lungs. Economic inactivity – like political apathy – is in some ways a rational response to an irrational situation, a society that has been complicit in its own mismanaged decline.

Writ large, the history of Wales is a salutary case study in what psychologists have come to know as the phenomenon of learned helplessness. When a human being or a social group is subjected to repeated setbacks that are beyond their immediate control, a natural emotional response is to become resigned to one's fate. Passivity in the face of adversity becomes the primary coping mechanism in situations of increasing stress – even when means of escaping the current situation present themselves. Inertia – political, economic, social – has its comforts, as does the victimhood complex that is as much a feature of nationalist thinking as Labour's familiar Tory-baiting narrative.

The antidote to learned helplessness is learned hopefulness, and the key to changing the way we think is to change the way we act. "Save the Welsh", wrote Nobel prize-winning economist Paul Krugman in his blog after a spectacularly inaccurate *New York Times* article on the Welsh economy. Well, I have news for the fact-checkers on the *New York Times*, and what is left of the newspaper industry at home. The only who ones who can save Wales are we, the Welsh, ourselves. There is no external salvation, no mythic *Mab Darogan* ('Son of Prophecy'), and every leather-jacketed hero will one day let you down. We, here, now – all of us, each of us – are the ones we have been waiting for.

Sadly, the official ideology that history has bequeathed us will not be a light unto our path. Labourism, like most unchallenged hegemonies, has ossified into a defensive monolith of a creed. It is a dead zone of ideas. Only the hopelessly deluded will think this power nexus can be challenged from the Right. What we need instead is some version of entrepreneurialism that is somehow consistent with the dominant Welsh values of equity and community. We need an economic autonomist movement that becomes as definitive to Welsh nationalism in the twenty-first century as the language movement was in the twentieth. This is not as hopelessly utopian as it may sound. Antonio Negri, the theorist of *operaismo*– that wonderfully sonorous term for the workers' self-management movement in his native Italy – has talked about the way Italian Leftists post-'68 moved their focus from politics to enterprise, both individual and social, seeding the economic dynamism of regions like Emilia-Romagna. What else, too, was Mondragon but Basque political action taking economic form?

A similar process was at work among those Welsh '68ers who started businesses, proclaiming their independence in the here-and-now – the young Dafydd Iwan and Sain, Robat Gruffudd at Y Lolfa, as well as co-operatives like Carl Clowes' Antur Aelhaearn. It can be seen in the decision of Dilys Davies, the clinical psychiatrist, not just to write about the need to raise Welsh self-confidence but to embody this in a business, Tro'r Trai ('Turning the Tide'), showing that Welsh culture, enterprise and tourism can be positively reinforcing.

Leanne Wood has called this approach 'real independence', to contrast it from the rather abstract notion – to most Welsh people at least – of juridical sovereignty. If independence is to be meaningful – particularly the 70%+ of employees who work in the private sector and for whom the Barnett Formula is a rather distant concern – then the real battle for control over our economic future is one being fought in the present tense. It is not enough to propose Welsh solutions to Welsh problems. We need to find Welsh solutions to global problems and then sell them to the world.

To be truly radical in a nation that has mistaken steady decline for stability and poverty for our birthright, we must become practical and prefigurative. We must create new enterprises and new communal and national institutions that cannot be swept away by bankers' fiat or political whim. We must awaken the spirit of what Kevin Morgan and I have elsewhere called 'The Collective Entrepreneur'.

In Wales this will mean a revolution in our thinking, but more importantly in our actions. This may lead to creative tension between the dominant traditions in our politics: the red and the green. But it could also mean a new synthesis. Frankly, I am agnostic on that.

What is certain is that we now need a new inflection point in our history. How soon is now?

5

When Adam
got in for Carmarthen

House of Commons – 12 July, 2001

THANK YOU, MR Deputy Speaker, for allowing me the opportunity to make my maiden speech today, a little later and a little hoarser – thanks to a bout of tonsillitis – than I had intended.

I, too, pay tribute to my predecessor. Dr Alan Williams was a most assiduous advocate on behalf of his constituents. A chemist, he brought to the House valuable expertise, a keen interest in scientific and environmental policy and a reasoned and logical approach to every issue that came to his attention. I wish him every success in future. Dr Williams had the honour to be the longest-serving Member of Parliament for a constituency renowned for febrile campaigning and unpredictability. Among my more colourful predecessors was William Paxton, who in his first attempt to capture the seat in 1802 kept the polls open for 15 days and bribed the electorate with 11,000 breakfasts, 36,000 dinners, 25,000 gallons of ale, 11,000 bottles of spirits – the list goes on – spending £18.18 on milk punch, whatever that is, and £786 on ribbons. He might have had a little difficulty explaining his actions to today's Electoral Commission.

The last Member of Parliament for the Carmarthen Boroughs seat was the nationalist and anti-Lloyd George Liberal Llewelyn Williams, who said of the House: "You get in to get on; you stay in to get honours; you get out to get honest." Perhaps his cynical view of politics can be explained by the rather curious Carmarthenshire tradition, which survived well into the twentieth century, whereby Tories wore red rosettes and their opponents blue – a tradition that in these days of ideological confusion seems strangely apt.

The political history of the Carmarthen constituency was especially interesting in the twentieth century. Carmarthen was the only Labour-held seat – apart from Mile End in London, which went Communist – that the party lost in the 1945 election. It was the only Labour-held seat that the party lost in the second 1974 election and on 7 June this year it became the only Labour-held seat lost in Wales.

Above all, Carmarthen was the first seat won by Plaid Cymru – the Party of Wales – in 1966. I pay special tribute to my predecessor Gwynfor Evans, the founder of modern Welsh nationalism. His integrity, eloquence and commitment to the cause of Wales set an example to which I can but hope to aspire. He continues to be an inspiration to everyone in my Party.

It is no exaggeration to say that the communities of East Carmarthen and Dinefwr have a unique, historic character. They stand on the cusp of rural and industrial Wales, and are the gateway to both. Four main valleys make up the constituency: the post-industrial Amman and Gwendraeth Valleys of the anthracite coalfield, and the agricultural heartlands of the Teifi and Tywi Valleys. The constituency has the only anthracite coalfield in Britain and produces more milk than any other county in the UK.

The interplay and interconnection of the two communities – the coalfield and the milkfield – lie at the heart of the special character of my constituency. The markets of the south Wales coalfield helped to build up the dairy sector. Welsh-speaking peasants and farmers, including my grandfather, huddled into the terraced cottages of the pit villages of Amman and Gwendraeth. Where others try to drive a wedge between town and country, we in Carmarthenshire have a bond of solidarity between village and valley, miner and farmer – from the free milk supplied by the farmers of Carmarthenshire to miners' families during the great strike of 1984, to the enormous concern shared by everyone in my constituency at the human cost of the deepening rural depression.

I was born and brought up in the industrial half of the constituency. My forefathers lived and worked in grim conditions, but they succeeded in sustaining a remarkably vibrant culture, which was characterised by a love of two languages, of religion and of all aspects of popular culture. That is certainly true of sport; the two valleys of Amman and Gwendraeth can boast the likes of Carwyn James, Barry John, Gareth Davies and Jonathan Davies – to name but a few of the greats of the Welsh game – as well as the emerging present-day talents of Shane Williams and Dwayne Peel. In snooker, we have in my constituency Matthew Stevens and Dominic Dale. In soccer, we have the former Welsh international goalkeeper, Dai Davies. Last but not least, my father was a former Welsh middleweight champion and, if I may say so, a formidable canvasser on the election trail.

Other great defining characteristics of the people of Carmarthenshire are their patriotism and democratic socialism. There was no finer an exponent of that than the late Jim Griffiths. Along with Aneurin Bevan, he was one of the two great founders of the welfare state, having introduced the National Insurance Act 1946 under the Attlee Government. He was also a firm believer in the Welsh dimension of politics, so it was fitting that he should have succeeded in being made the Charter Secretary of State for Wales – a fulfilment of his lifelong ambition for his country. He passionately believed – as I do today – that the villages and valleys had something distinctive to contribute to our shared humanity.

The essence of these values was captured in, of all places, last Friday's edition of *The Times*, in an obituary of the theologian W D Davies, who was originally from Glanaman. "Davies," it said, "had the quiet dignity of the miners he knew as a child, people who knew the depth of economic depression but retained the self-respect that they found in the Christian faith. The social values of the Nonconformist chapels of the Amman Valley gave him a concern for those he perceived as victims, and this developed into a natural affinity with the Jewish people." Jim Griffiths was a product of that same tradition, but in the 1960s the vision and the values on which such great communities had been built were threatened – ironically as a result of his own government's policies.

In an archive in Ammanford, there is a letter written by Jim Griffiths to a Labour Party colleague shortly after the 1966 Carmarthen by-election, stating baldly that all Labour seats in Wales were vulnerable. Jim Griffiths' particular concern was that the Labour Party had lost the support of young people. The cause was clear then as it is now. As Gwynfor Evans declared in his maiden speech 35 years ago, "The Labour Party boasts of prosperity but the people of Carmarthen see no evidence of this prosperity. What they see is mines closing, railways closing, steel workers being made redundant and a decline in agriculture." The parallel between those words, spoken 35 years ago, with the Wales of today is chilling in its accuracy.

The Labour Party has never really recaptured the energies of young people in Wales. That is why I stand here a Plaid Member, a miner's son and the youngest Member representing a Welsh constituency. When hubris threatens to overwhelm some of my fellow Welshmen on the government benches, perhaps they should ask themselves why people of my generation and background have turned their backs on Labour.

The issue of post-16 education possibly offers some clues. There are few issues that for me define more precisely the essence of social justice in an advanced society than access to education. Further and higher education were to me, as to so many Hon. Members, the key that unlocked the door to the favoured position that we now enjoy.

Education involves not only individual benefit but social and economic gain for society as a whole. Indeed, according to the recent report by the Organisation for Economic Co-operation and Development, almost half a percentage point of the annual average growth rate in the UK in the 1990s was due to educational attainment. More sobering was the finding in the report that, in 1998, the UK spent only 4.9% of gross domestic product on education compared with an OECD average of 5.3% – still far below the Scandinavian countries and New Zealand, which invest more than 7% of their annual income on education.

Alongside questions of funding lies the issue of student financial support, on which the Opposition is curiously silent. Like many an Hon. Member, my training ground for political engagement was the National Union of Students. I particularly remember the presidential term of the Hon. Member for Enfield, Southgate (Mr Twigg) and the great lobby of Westminster against student loans, which ended in deadlock – unfortunately – on Westminster Bridge.

Our policy in the NUS was to defend and extend the principle of the maintenance grant to embrace all those in full-time post-16 education. Our fears then about the effects of the abolition of the maintenance grant have been borne out by a string of recent reports. The Higher Education Funding Council for Wales last year published research showing that, following the introduction of student fees, prospective students from the deprived communities of south Wales were up to three times less likely to attend university.

Earlier this year, the Rees report on student hardship,

commissioned by the Lib-Lab coalition in the National Assembly, echoed the Cubie report in calling for the abolition of tuition fees and went further in calling for a statutory entitlement to maintenance support for all those in HE and FE. That was the very same policy that many of us were advocating back in the 1980s while in the NUS.

As the youngest of three working-class children to go to university, and one of the last to receive a full maintenance grant, I am passionately committed to ensuring that the same opportunities are afforded to today's generation of young people. Passion in politics, it seems, is no bad thing – even, if the House will forgive me, in a maiden speech.

It is often said that the difference between a Llanelli and a Swansea supporter – those two great rivals of west Wales rugby – is that Swansea supporters wear gloves and Llanelli supporters cannot afford them. I am a Llanelli supporter through and through and I assure the House that my gloves will be off in many of our debates – not out of any enmity for Labour Members, but because I care so deeply about a special place that I love and a special people whom I love. Their demands over the twentieth century were modest, but their contribution was immense. They deserve a future that is better than the past. It is our collective duty to ensure that it is delivered.

6

High crimes and misdemeanours

House of Commons – 26 August, 2004

NEW LABOUR, NEW politics – that was the promise. In Blair's own words in his first speech as leader to the Labour Party conference, "It means being open. It means telling it like it is. Let's be honest. Straight. Those most in need of hope deserve the truth."

Now, almost a decade later, his words sound like self-parody. And yet there remains a certain resonance about them. Truth is the foundation of democracy. Without truth, there can be no trust, and without trust, politics loses its very legitimacy. And that is the tragedy of what has befallen us all in the last three years of this premiership – alongside the personal tragedies of the 64 British service personnel and 13,000 Iraqis who have paid the highest price for what has become the cruellest of deceptions.

Faced with this charge of having duped us into war, the Prime Minister responds with a certain injured innocence: "Are people questioning my integrity? Are they saying I lied?" Of course, professional communicators such as the Prime

Minister almost never tell lies. For the most part it's perfectly easy to mislead the public without resorting to that. As Robin Cook wrote in his diary, Blair was "far too clever" for that. Rather than allege there was a real link between Saddam and Bin Laden, "he deliberately crafted a suggestive phrase designed to create the impression that British troops were going to Iraq to fight a threat from al-Qaida".

There is more than one way not to tell the truth: half-truths, omissions and deliberate ambiguities can be just as effective as crude lies if the mission is to mislead. All this would still be in the realm of conjecture, of course, if it had not been for the death of David Kelly and Bush's decision to have his own inquiry. Without these unforeseen events, we would never have had access to the information revealed through the Butler and Hutton inquiries.

But we do. We now know what Blair knew and when he knew it, and the contrast with his public statements at the time, which are set out in the report, *A Case To Answer*, by Dan Plesch and Glen Rangwala, published today. On the basis of that report, I am prepared to state – unprotected by parliamentary privilege, unfettered by the rules of parliamentary language and without equivocation – that the Prime Minister did not tell the truth. Instead he exaggerated, distorted, suppressed and manipulated the information for political ends. This was an organised deception to win over a sceptical Parliament and public to the military action he had long ago promised his ally Mr Bush.

The evidence for Blair's duplicity is overwhelming. He claimed in early 2002 that Iraq had "stockpiles of major amounts of chemical and biological weapons", while the assessment of the joint intelligence committee at the time was that Iraq "may have hidden small quantities of agents and weapons". He told the TUC in September 2002 that Saddam "had enough chemical and biological weapons remaining to devastate the entire Gulf region", while the intelligence assessment was that "Saddam has not succeeded in seriously threatening his neighbours".

71

Blair displayed the most despicable cynicism of all when he warned that "it is a matter of time, unless we act and take a stand, before terrorism and weapons of mass destruction come together", even though the Government was later forced to admit to the Butler Review that "the Joint Intelligence Committee assessed that any collapse of the Iraqi regime would increase the risk of chemical and biological warfare technology or agents finding their way into the hands of terrorists, and that the Prime Minister was aware of this". He knew the nightmare scenario he painted would be more, not less, likely if we invaded Iraq, yet he gave the opposite impression to translate anxiety into support for the war.

If he was guilty of mismanagement, miscalculation or mere mistakes, then the proper place to hold him to account would be the ballot box. Deliberate misrepresentation, however, is what marks this Prime Minister out. When Peter Mandelson caused "incorrect information" to be given to the House, and Beverley Hughes admitted giving a "misleading impression", they resigned in accordance with the ministerial code, which states: "Ministers who knowingly mislead Parliament will be expected to offer their resignation to the Prime Minister". Unfortunately, the code is silent on what to do with a miscreant prime minister.

His refusal to resign in the face of such evidence is unprecedented. There are strong indications, detailed in the report, that he made a secret agreement with President Bush, which is illegal under constitutional law. Yet there are to be no further enquiries, no further comment from the Prime Minister, and no hope of ever seeing the Attorney General's full advice. A motion of no confidence would simply divide the House on party lines and fail to focus on the actions of Blair. And, as John Baron MP recently discovered, accusing another member of misleading the House is deemed 'unparliamentary'.

Accountability is the lifeblood of democracy. Why should the public bother getting involved in politics if ministers can lead us into war on a false prospectus and not even utter a single word of apology? So what remedy do Parliament and people have in these desperate circumstances? Historically, impeachment has been used by Parliament against individuals to punish "high crimes and misdemeanours".

One MP is all it takes to make the accusation of high crimes and misdemeanours against a public official for an impeachment process to begin. Once an MP has presented his or her evidence of misconduct to the Commons in a debate, and if a majority of elected members agree there is a case to answer, a committee of MPs is established to draw up articles of impeachment, which will list each charge individually. The case goes before the Lords.

Three centuries ago, the Commons called impeachment "the chief institution for the preservation of the government". It has been a key weapon in the long struggle of Parliament against the abuse of executive power. It has been revived before, after long periods of disuse, when the executive's hold on power-without-responsibility seemed every bit as total as today.

Today a number of MPs, including myself, are declaring our intention to bring a Commons motion of impeachment against the Prime Minister in relation to the invasion of Iraq. This is the first time in more than 150 years that such a motion has been brought against a Minister of the Crown, and it is clearly not an undertaking we enter into lightly. We do it with regret, but also with resolve. For our first duty is to the people we represent, who feel they were misled, whose trust was betrayed, who have been placed in harm's way by the irresponsible actions of this Prime Minister. It is in their name that we impeach him. It is in their name, and with all the authority vested in us, that we implore him now to go.

7

We fought a war over an arsenal of non-existent weapons

House of Commons, Iraq War Inquiry debate – 31 October, 2006

That this House believes that there should be a select committee of seven honourable Members, being members of Her Majesty's Privy Council, to review the way in which the responsibilities of Government were discharged in relation to Iraq and all matters relevant thereto, in the period leading up to military action in that country in March 2003 and in its aftermath.

IT IS AN honour to move this motion on behalf of my Hon. Friends and of right Hon. and Hon. Members on all sides of the House of Commons. It is the culmination of a long campaign, and it is a debate that is long overdue. The motion has cross-party support because the issue at its heart is far bigger than one of party politics. It is about accountability. It is about the monumental catastrophe of the Iraq war, which is the worst foreign-policy disaster certainly since Suez, and possibly since

Munich. It is about the morass in which, regrettably, we still find ourselves. It is also about a breakdown in our system of government – a fault line in our constitution that only we, as Parliament, can fix. Fix it we must, if there are not to be further mistakes and other Iraqs under other prime ministers, in which case we shall only have ourselves to blame.

The debate on 18 March 2003 was one of the most momentous – some would say most calamitous – debates in the House of Commons in modern times. The Prime Minister gave one of the great performances of his life; it was full of certainty and undaunted by doubt. But unfortunately, we now know that much of what he told us that night was false. It is no wonder that democratic politics has haemorrhaged public confidence. Only we in this Parliament can stem that flow; we can rebuild some of that trust by holding a proper inquiry into what went on.

What could an inquiry usefully do? There will inevitably be a range of views within the House, which is why we need a sufficiently broad remit. But three central questions need to be answered. How could the Government take us to war on claims that turned out to be false? When precisely was the decision to have this war made? Why has the planning for, and conduct of, the occupation proved to be so disastrous?

Almost on a weekly basis, we see senior military figure after senior military figure making yet another devastating assessment of the Government's policy-making capacity. Lord Guthrie said that the policies are cuckoo. Lord Inge said that there was a lack of clear strategy at the Ministry of Defence. Most damning of all was the verdict of the current head of the Army [General Sir Richard Dannatt], who said that:

> history will show that the planning for what happened after the initial… war fighting phase was poor, probably based more on optimism than sound planning.

Unfortunately, we have not seen that kind of honesty from any

Government minister to date. However, it is fair to say that the Foreign Secretary came perilously close when she said that history may judge the Iraq war to have been a disaster. Unfortunately, we do not have the luxury of waiting for history's verdict; we need some answers and action now.

A Government who were prepared to parade before our eyes dossier after dodgy dossier of carefully edited intelligence will not now let us read any of the intelligence on what is happening on the ground. We have had no comprehensive statement to date of Government policy. In February last year, the Prime Minister promised the Liaison Committee that General Luck's audit of coalition security strategy in Iraq would be published. For the record, I quote the Prime Minister:

> I have seen a draft that is still under discussion... When there is a finished article, it will be published.

It never was.

Before the Government come back and say, "That was not our fault; the decision not to publish was made in Washington" – like so many other foreign policy decisions under this Government – I should point out to Treasury ministers that they have not published a single word of Sir Ronnie Flanagan's assessment of the UK's contribution to Iraqi security sector reform, which was completed 10 months ago. Of course we understand that parts of these reports have to be withheld for security reasons, but does the Foreign Secretary really believe that Parliament can do its duty in holding the Government to account if we get no information about their strategy?

There are two Iraqs: the Iraq of George Bush and the Prime Minister, where things are going to plan and getting better all the time; and the real Iraq of murder and mayhem, whose future is uncertain. The state of denial that characterises the Government's policy now mirrors the state of delusion that characterised their policy in the run-up to war. The Prime Minister told us that night that it was "beyond doubt" that Iraq had weapons of mass destruction, even though the intelligence supplied was packed with doubt. He rattled off the huge quantities of weapons of mass destruction (WMD) that he said had been left unaccounted for. Then he treated us to the punchline:

> We are asked now seriously to accept that in the last few years – contrary to all history, contrary to all intelligence – Saddam decided unilaterally to destroy those weapons. I say that such a claim is palpably absurd.

Well, not as things turned out. In my more uncharitable moments, I am reminded of that famous put-down by Aneurin Bevan during the Suez crisis. He said, "If Sir Anthony Eden is sincere in what he is saying – and he may be, he may be – then he is too stupid to be Prime Minister." I should like to state as a matter of record that I do not believe that the Prime Minister is stupid; that is a wholly unwarranted and unfounded accusation.

I want to return to some of the Prime Minister's statements that were out of kilter with much of what he was being told. To give just one example, on 3 April 2002 he said, "We know that he" – Saddam Hussein – *"has stockpiles of major amounts of chemical and biological weapons."*

But in the previous month, the most that the Joint Intelligence Committee could come up with was:

> We believe Iraq retains some production equipment, and some small stocks of chemical warfare agent precursors, and may have hidden small quantities of agents and weapons.

So "may" became "we know" and "small quantities" became "major stockpiles"; that was the pattern in the presentation of the case. Small changes in emphasis and the selective use of intelligence were repeatedly used to transform a threat from minor to dire and doubtful to definite, and caveats and caution to blood-chilling certainties.

Evidence that would have undermined the case was held back. The Prime Minister frequently cited the defection of Hussein Kamel, Saddam Hussein's son-in-law, and his admission in 1995 that Iraq had indeed had an extensive WMD programme. However, what the Prime Minister omitted to tell the House was that Hussein Kamel also told UN inspectors in 1995 that he had personally ordered the destruction of all biological, chemical and nuclear weapons, and that that had happened.

Most indefensible of all was justification of the war in Iraq on the basis that it would reduce the likelihood of a terrorist attack, even though the intelligence services were saying the opposite at the time.

Jeremy Corbyn – Labour, Islington North:

Does the Hon. Gentleman also concede that any inquiry should look in some detail at the circumstances under which the UN weapons inspectors, led by Hans Blix, were withdrawn from Iraq in January 2003 and not allowed to go back, having confirmed that they believed with 99% certainty that there were no such weapons of mass destruction in Iraq?

Adam Price:

Absolutely. I entirely agree with the Hon. Gentleman.

As we have learned over the past few days, with the leaked Cabinet minutes and the leaked National Intelligence Estimate from the United States, the invasion of Iraq has increased the threat of terrorist attacks. It is a sad indictment of the Government that we learn more from leaked Cabinet papers than we ever do from a Cabinet minister speaking at the Dispatch Box. I hope that this afternoon will be an exception.

Another critical issue surrounded by confusion and controversy was the timing of the decision to go to war. We were told right up to the last few days before the debate in the House that no decision had been taken, but there is now compelling evidence that the Prime Minister had already made a decision to invade a year earlier. As early as March 2002, the Prime Minister's foreign policy adviser, Sir David Manning, was assuring Condoleezza Rice of the Prime Minister's unbudgeable support for regime change. Days later, Sir Christopher Meyer sent a dispatch to Downing Street detailing how he repeated that commitment to the US Deputy Defence Secretary. The Ambassador added that the Prime Minister would need a cover for military action: "I then went through the need to wrong-foot Saddam on the inspectors and the UN Security Council resolutions." Yet throughout that period, the Prime Minister was insisting that the war was not inevitable and no decision had been made.

Most incredibly of all, in the most recent leaked memorandum, we read that, in a meeting with the Prime Minister, the President even suggested provoking a war with Saddam by flying a US spy plane bearing UN colours over Iraq and enticing the Iraqis to take a shot at it. That is the clearest suggestion yet that the UN was being used not to prevent war, but as a pretext for beginning it.

There is no shame in changing one's mind when new facts come to light. Ask the Attorney General. He changed his mind three times in three weeks. He finally decided on 13 March 2003, after talking things through with his secretary, that his 7 March opinion was wrong after all and that, to quote the Attorney General's recent disclosure to the Information Commissioner, *"the better view was that a further resolution was not legally necessary"*.

Incredibly, that U-turn was not based on a detailed paper setting out the legal arguments. The Attorney General, who, by his own admission, is not an expert in international law, did not ask for legal advice until after he had come to his decision. *[Interruption.]* The Minister is shaking his head. I am reading from the Government's own disclosure to the Information Commissioner, which states:

> It was also decided to prepare a statement setting out the
> Attorney's view of the legal position and to send instructions to
> counsel to help in the preparation of that public statement.

So the Attorney General decided what the legal position was, and then asked for legal advice. You could not make it up, Mr Speaker – well, you could if you were the Attorney General, apparently.

The Attorney General went on in the same disclosure statement to admit, crucially, that the revival argument – the notion that the use of force authorised by Resolution 678 from the First Gulf War was capable of being revived by the Security Council – "was and remains controversial". Finally, a full three years on from the invasion, we have an unequivocal admission from the Attorney General in his statement to the House that the war was legal was "controversial" – his word, not mine.

There is a fundamental breakdown at the heart of the Government that is continuing to affect decisions that are being made now. The Government have made a catalogue of errors that have resulted in problems on the ground. As Hon. Members have said, the problem was that we had not government by Cabinet, but government by cabal. The delicate checks and balances of our constitution were swept away. Cabinet was sidelined and Parliament was misled...

There is a problem at the heart of our constitution and tonight we need to reapply the constitutional brakes. The military men have been lining up to criticise and so have the mandarins. A letter from Sir Michael Quinlan – of all people – a former Permanent Secretary at the Ministry of Defence, said that the Prime Minister:

> exerted or connived... to mould legal advice to his preference
> and failed to disclose fully... even that moulded advice; and... so
> arranged the working of the Cabinet that colleagues had no timely
> or systematic opportunity to consider the merits of his policy in an
> informed manner.

Lord Butler made the same point in an interview in *The Spectator*. He pointed out that decisions were made on the prime ministerial sofa, rather than in meetings with minutes around the Cabinet table, with all that that meant for both the quality of, and proper accountability for, decision making. Pluralism in the Government, a proper role for Parliament and the Cabinet and a truly independent civil service are there to act as a check on hubris in government. That is why we need to recalibrate the constitution of this United Kingdom and rebalance power for the benefit of Parliament, at the expense of an over-mighty Executive. We are otherwise reduced to the sorry spectacle of an Attorney General changing his mind to save his political master's skin.

Let us remind ourselves once again of the central fact: we fought the war because of an arsenal of weapons that proved to be non-existent. Many thousands of people have paid with their lives for that mistake, and the same mirage of deception and disinformation continues to cloud our understanding of what is happening on the ground.

The constant hailing of non-existent progress by the Government is an insult to those who genuinely appreciate what is really happening in a worsening situation. It is a scandal that, as yet, not a single minister has unequivocally admitted that things in Iraq have gone wrong. Both in the run-up to the war and in its aftermath, the Government's policy has been characterised by a cocktail of wishful thinking, self-delusion and evasion. The sequence of events that led us to commit our armed forces to a war that was illegal and unnecessary is as yet unexplained. The strategy for removing them remains unpublished. The inquiry we are calling for is not only essential to understanding what happened three and a half years ago; it is imperative in understanding where we go from here. It is impossible truly to discern the problems on the ground in Iraq unless we appreciate what went wrong – the mistakes and misjudgments that took us there in the first place.

History does not repeat itself, as Mark Twain once said, but it does rhyme. Fifty years ago today, our Government began bombing Egypt under the cover of darkness. That invasion, too, was based on a falsehood. Anthony Eden secretly colluded with Israel and France, and kept Parliament in the dark. It is a matter of debate as to whether the Prime Minister deliberately deceived us, but one way or another we were certainly misled. The evidence clearly suggests that he had privately assured President Bush that he would join the invasion. Here was a Prime Minister so deluded by his determination to do what he believed to be right that he began to think not as *primus inter pares* but as an acting head of state. It is time now to tell the Prime Minister and all future prime ministers that they are not presidents, and that the policy of this United Kingdom does not always have to be the policy of the United States.

8

A bittersweet farewell

Leaving Dinner, House of Commons – March 2010

I LEAVE THIS place with feelings as bittersweet as the last course in this last supper... Of course, if you do not feel frustrated at Westminster then you probably shouldn't be here – at least not as a Welsh Nationalist. To walk these corridors of power is to be sandwiched between the brainwashed of New Labour and the brain-dead of the Conservatives.

I have done my nine years of National Service – and I am nothing but full of admiration for those that will continue to serve – to my mind, beyond the call of duty.

In these days of disillusionment, what people in our movement must always remember is that the cause to which we are called is that most noble of all causes: the liberty and dignity of our people, and of all the peoples on this earth. Where others see Wales and the world as it is, and ask 'Why?', we dream of a Wales and a world that has never yet been, and we ask 'Why Not?'

It's a life after politics for me now. I was looking the other day for some ideas as to what I might do next and I see that George W Bush is now a motivational speaker. I guess that would work. He started two wars and plunged the world into a depression. Compared to him, anyone's going to feel good about themselves.

I am not going to America to escape – but to find new inspiration – a space and time to think. And where better to seek that inspiration than Massachussetts, the home of the lion of the Senate, the late, great Ted Kennedy.

9

Declaration of Independence

Harvard University Commencement Speech – 26 May, 2011

IN HARVARD YARD in 1775 George Washington's army was housed here in Hollis Hall, wracked by exhaustion and fear, sustained only by coffee, canteen food and the promise of future happiness – it sounds a bit like finals week. Lined up on the opposite bank of the Charles River were hundreds of my Welsh ancestors, the Royal Welch Fusiliers, fighting for the British Army against the American Revolution. I should apologize really. You seem to have made a success of this independence thing. Well done, and thanks for leaving us Canada.

But the people I think about most today are my Welsh ancestors that were on *this* side of the river, fighting for the revolution. Who showed an independence of mind whose spirit I want to invoke today. Fourteen of the signers of the American Declaration of Independence were Welsh, who had found here, like me at Harvard, a space to think and chart their own course. Who were inspired by the dream of freedom, first forged here, that is still troubling tyrants from Tripoli to Damascus.

Unlike the hidebound British, who never broke ranks, the American Revolutionaries knew the value of fighting for each other, yet thinking for themselves. They struck out on their own, and built something new together. Today we are bathed in a sea of black and crimson, but in this university of knowledge lies a diversity of understanding. In the 133 countries represented here today, and from the proud peacock blue of the Kennedy School to the canary yellow of Design, the deep red of Divinity and the purple of Law, it is our differences that give us our distinction.

Yet we live in a world of creeping homogenization. A blue planet that is becoming small and grey. Where a language is set to die every fourteen days; where globalization puts a Starbucks at every street corner; where Google has made the transfer of knowledge as easy as the click of a mouse – how else would we have finished our dissertations? Are we all slowly beginning to speak, to see, to sound the same? And even to think alike?

In one recent study, half of all college students showed no improvement in their capacity for independent thinking by the end of their sophomore year. Even while sober. It's nothing new. Fifty years ago Yale psychologist Stanley Milgram showed us how dangerous and pervasive conformity could be: 65% of people in his famous experiment were prepared to inflict an electric shock when asked to do so. But then what else do you do for entertainment in New Haven on a Tuesday night?

At its best, the university is the incubator of independent inquiry, a cacophony of voices, opinions, arguments, a living debate that reshapes us as we shape it. But here's the irony: that to graduate we must first master the established theories. So though we are meant to stand here on the shoulders of giants, it can sometimes feel as if that body of accumulated learning, all the tried and tested frameworks and formulas, are weighing down upon us, crushing our creativity. And threaten to sink us if we are not careful.

In a world where the deepest problems defy easy resolution, surely the greatest risk is not taking risks at all. So will we have the courage to mount our own quiet revolution? Generations ago, there was an army of people, drawn here from many lands, who rejected the status quo. Who turned their world upside down. So today let's salute them: the dissenters, the mavericks and heretics, the pioneers and prime movers, who know that without being willing to risk being wrong, we can never be right. That only by questioning what is can we begin to imagine what might be. That it's in our originality that we will find humanity's greatest hope.

The world needs less of the same. It needs us to work together and think for ourselves. It needs the commonwealth of us and the republic of you. Let's make today our independence day, and in our liberty, strive to serve the common good.

10

Democratic deficit

The Welsh Agenda – Spring 2005

DEVOLUTION WAS MEANT to be the catalyst for a new politics. It was meant to address the democratic deficit of falling turnouts and disillusionment with a government that was over-bearing and remote. It was going to change the relationship between the government and the governed. What is clear now is that devolution has not transformed the culture of politics. It has simply shown up its weaknesses.

The Assembly, like the Westminster Parliament, is largely powerless against an unchecked Executive. Elected members see themselves as bound by the party line, not as individual representatives following their conscience or the interests of their constituents. Centralism, spin and the urge to control remain the hallmarks of political style. The inclusivity which was meant to be one of the design principles of the Assembly has been long forgotten in the rush to the comforting familiarity of the Westminster model. But instead of resulting in a separation of powers, as is often argued, the result has been a further concentration in the hands of the Executive.

To understand the confusion, you have to go back into parliamentary history. Separation of powers was first mooted by Clement Walker, a member of the Long Parliament in 1648, as a guarantee against the kind of arbitrary, tyrannical rule against which the governed had to be protected. The remedy he suggested lay in a separation of governmental functions between the "Governing power", the "Legislative power", and the "Judicative power".

What subsequently developed was a constitutional system in which King and Parliament were limited by the authority of the other, the system of checks and balances lauded by Montesquieu and admired by the framers of the American Constitution. However, with the growth of prime ministerial power, the Executive has increasingly dominated the legislature, and to some extent the judiciary, because of its monopoly over the lawmaking process.

So in slavishly adopting a parliamentary model, the Assembly has imported all the worst features of the Westminster charade: the near-complete concentration of power in the hands of the Executive, with an Assembly symbolically important, but in reality increasingly irrelevant.

The most bitter betrayal of all of the new politics we thought we were building must be the calculated attack we have seen on the idea of proportional representation: "The absence of first-past-the-post in Wales and Scotland will by itself promote a more pluralistic politics since it will be less easy for a single party to secure an overall majority, and so will encourage government by partnership." So said the Secretary of State [Peter Hain] in 2000 about an electoral system he now describes as fatally flawed.

For all the hopeful talk of plugging the democratic deficit, of building a laboratory of democracy, we are still concentrating in the hands of the few all the short-term authority taken from the many. Instead of the radical experimentalism of a decentred democracy, with its overlapping and competing sovereignties, we have the conformity and single-mindedness of indivisible power and a permanent majority. What I would call, half jokingly – though only half – the dictatorship of the Cabinet secretariat.

If I sound a little negative, it's because I think we are in a very negative phase in Welsh politics, when quangos are abolished and New Labour nostrums roundly rejected, but nobody's very clear about what we're going to put in their place. The few policy innovations of the Welsh Assembly Government – free prescriptions, free breakfasts and free swimming lessons – are, at best, very modest in their scope. As Rosa Luxemburg wrote in the context of the Russian revolution, "The negative, the tearing down can be decreed; the building up, the positive cannot." Kafka, I think, captured the same sense of dejection that many of us who campaigned for the Yes vote in 1997 now inevitably feel: "The revolution has evaporated and all that remains is the mud of a new bureaucracy."

So how can we reverse our own slide into bureaucratic centralism? First of all, we could extend and deepen democracy throughout the public sphere, and adopt the American practice of directly electing a much wider array of public officials. American citizens elect virtually everyone, from the district attorney to the chief of police, the head of the fire department and the local school board. Coupled with the recall principle, this produces a much greater sense of real accountability.

In the light of the appalling failures of representative democracy to get to grips with the crisis in the NHS, there is a strong case for introducing a participatory element through electing the chairs of the local health boards. This is preferable to the elections for foundation hospital trusts being trialled in England, because ordinary people don't want a say in how hospitals are run. Their objective is that the hospital delivers the goods and services they want. And it's creating a democratically elected body to plan services that's key to that, rather than re-establishing the pre-NHS voluntary hospital principle, or retaining the powerless community health councils which were abolished in England. This would evaluate performance against the public interest – as a sort of permanent whistle-blower with privileged access to internal documents and discussions. In this way we might have avoided the communications breakdown that appeared to build up in the run-up to the Welsh Development Agency's demise. This, to my mind, would be a far better guarantee of transparency and accountability than taking an agency inside Government.

More radical still perhaps, would be the idea of a Citizen's Assembly: sixty people, chosen randomly like a jury, to sit for a month as a committee of the entire nation, a radical revising chamber, representing every part of Wales, all walks of life. How would it work? Well, using the techniques of deliberative democracy, they could be asked to decide whether to pass into law certain Assembly initiatives – no more than one or two – which had been referred to them by a third of the directly elected Assembly members. It may seem a pretty bold idea. But, with the collapse in trust and popular engagement, we need to start using our imaginative faculties.

We will soon have an empty debating chamber in Crickhowell House. Why not use it to let the people in? I think it would reconnect people to our democracy. People would identify with ordinary people weighing up the pros and cons of difficult decisions in a 'Big Brother house' of democracy. And if people doubt the ability of 60 ordinary Welsh women and men, they should read *The Wisdom of Crowds* by James Surowiecki. Groups of ordinary people are smarter than individual experts, no matter how brilliant. They are better at solving problems, fostering innovation, coming to wise decisions, and even predicting the future.

11

The red-green grass of home: in support of a Plaid / Labour alliance

The Welsh Agenda – 6 June, 2007

PEOPLE MAY BE surprised that after weeks sweating blood over the All-Wales Accord, I am still a red-green enthusiast. So let me briefly outline my reasons why.

Reason 1

Plaid and Labour, despite their bitter disagreements over the national question and over much else besides, do still both stem from the Welsh radical tradition with its emphasis on egalitarianism, the values of community, solidarity and progressive universalism and Rawlsian notions of social justice. The reason that many of us (though by no means all) were drawn to Plaid in the first place was not out of an abstract belief in self-government per se, but our conviction that only through self-government could these ideals be fulfilled by banishing forever the prospect of a right-wing London government (whether Tory or New Labour) imposing its alien values on

Wales. A red-green realignment of the Welsh left – the bringing together of the traditions of Gwynfor Evans and Jim Griffiths, of D J Davies and S O Davies – is something of which many of us have long dreamed.

Reason 2

Moving forward to the next stage of self-government – by holding a referendum on a Welsh Parliament as set out in the Government of Wales Act 2006 – requires the support of 40 AMs, which is not possible without at least some Labour support. Winning that referendum would require the active support of the Labour Party as a whole, otherwise it would be 1979 all over again, not 1997.

Reason 3

An agreement with Plaid would weaken the Monmouthshire-and-Merthyr chauvinists within the Labour Party and strengthen the Welsh progressive wing. The new Conservative ascendancy at Westminster post-2009 would help create the conditions for a new red-green consensus in Wales which would propel Wales on an accelerated path to self-government.

A red-green alliance is not without its risks, however. For us as the Official Opposition, to cede our right to form an alternative government to a lacklustre Labour administration that promises little more than four more years of drift would be disastrous for Welsh democracy. We would need hard evidence that the Labour Party in Wales is *genuinely* committed to change. Which is why we need to set out three clear conditions for our support for a Labour First Minister:

Condition 1

It has to be a full formal Coalition with Plaid Cymru ministers in the Cabinet. The New Zealand model of 'confidence and supply' may be appropriate in the case of a tiny opposition party offering one or two seats to get a ruling party over the finishing line. It is not appropriate for the Official Opposition being asked to forgo the chance of forming its own administration and give the ruling party carte blanche for four years. We are talking here about a Grand Coalition arrangement as with the CDU-CSU and the SPD in Germany, or the People's Party and the Social Democrats in Austria. Nothing else is acceptable.

Condition 2

Instead of a few nods to the Plaid manifesto, a Labour-Plaid Coalition Government would have to agree on an entire programme of government for the full four-year term. We desperately need the kind of exciting, visionary ideas that we see in the All-Wales Accord if we are to re-engender some enthusiasm for devolution among the Welsh people again. Under Rhodri Morgan, Labour have become a conservative, managerialist administration. If we simply have the status quo for four years, then a referendum on further powers will be lost. Labour needs Plaid in government to inject some fresh thinking, creativity and inspiration.

Condition 3

A referendum on law-making powers must be held within the four-year term, with active Labour Party support.

If these three conditions are met, then I would support a red-green alternative as would, I believe, a majority of my Party's National Council.

But an invisible clock is ticking. Rhodri Morgan needs to make that call. Soon it could be too late and Labour will have no-one to blame but themselves for being out of power for a generation.

[The 'One Wales' Accord between Labour and Plaid Cymru at the National Assembly was agreed on 27 June 2007]

12

Democratic socialism and the people

Blog post – 5 July, 2007

A LOT OF discussion in nationalist blogs and within online communities like maes-e recently has focused on whether and why Plaid Cymru is a party of the Left. Some have seen this as some kind of sentimental attachment to an imagined and idealised past of working-class radicalism. Coming from a totally different direction, Kim Howells has also attacked what he sees as the proto-nationalist myth of *y werin* ('the common people', as opposed to the gentry).

So what does socialism signify in the modern Wales? Well, to me it is more than some kind of fashionable label – nor am I particularly hung-up about the s-word per se, though it was invented by a Welshman and is still the best shorthand to describe the set of values that define the democratic left. But what does it actually stand for? Well, here's my attempt at a short manifesto of the modern Welsh left, to which others will inevitably add theirs.

The freedom to flourish as individuals can only be built on a foundation of equality. We therefore commit ourselves to a Wales which is governed in the interests of the least well-off, not the wealthiest. Social justice, equality and the fullest development of people's potential are our aims, and the means of their achievement is the democratic self-government of our nation, its economy, society and cultural life.

We should aim to spread aspiration and opportunity to every level of Welsh society. There should be no limits to people's dreams for themselves, their families, their community or their nation – only the need to share with others the fruits of their success.

While markets are crucial in driving forward creativity, innovation and entrepreneurialism, many of the challenges that we will face in the twenty-first century can only be addressed by us working together as citizens, not as individual customers. From transport to public services, from community safety to the environment and democracy itself – these are all public goods that cannot be adequately provided by the market – but only collectively, as a community.

Our vision is not just of managing Wales and the wider world but of transforming them for the benefit of future generations and the majority of our people. Not just of attending to the urgent problems of the present, but of sowing the seeds of our shared future.

Making progress and moving forward. Together.

13

Reinventing radical Wales

Abridged version of a chapter in *Politics in 21st Century Wales* (IWA, 2008)

> The forces with the best chance to achieve and maintain political predominance in the near future of the advanced societies are those – whether right, centre or left – that most persuasively associate themselves with the cause of restless experimentation and energy. It matters to the future of these societies that they also be forces committed to the belief that the freedom of some depends on the emancipation of all.
>
> Roberto Unger

I HAVE, FOR as long as I can remember, had the habit of reading books backwards. From a very young age it struck me that only through realising how a story ends could you truly understand the meaning of its beginning. The same principle, of course, applies to history. As the Austrian economist Joseph Schumpeter once remarked, political events seldom reveal their true significance within the same decade. There can be no arguments that the Days of May (2007) were among the most dramatic in recent Welsh history. The Celtic Spring writ large – with nationalists in power in each of the three Celtic corners of this for-now-at-least-still-United Kingdom – is already seen as a defining moment in the story of these islands. But what the moment means is still being worked out. It depends on what happens next.

The wait to be vindicated by events will undoubtedly weigh on my Party more heavily than on all others because in choosing to enter into coalition with our principal political opponents, we effectively entered into what Gwyn Alf Williams would have recognised as a Pascal's Wager on the future of Wales. As a historical political reality, Wales can still be a characterised as a tentative, emerging nation. The role of a nationalist party in these circumstances is to force the pace of change: to act prefiguratively, or, as the Scottish novelist Alasdair Gray has put it so memorably, "to work as if you live in the early days of a better nation".

Being a Welsh nationalist used to require heroic reserves of patience. Like revolutionaries the world over, we were always waiting for that Great Leap Forward, while busying ourselves with the politics of small steps – little victories, heroic defeats, principled stands – but never quite the 'Free Wales' which always seemed just out of our grasp. Now we are transformed from a party of struggle to a party of struggle in government, we can practise impatience instead, not through protest but through policy. If Wales is a *verspätete Nation*, a late developer in Marxist terms, then now at least we get to put our shoulders to the wheel.

It is a lamentable fact, of course, but the Government of Wales Act 2006 bestowed upon us the slowest form of government in the world. It is, in Edwin Morgan's phrase, "a symposium of procrastinators". A policy must first be adopted by a political party in its manifesto, supported by the electorate, included in a Government programme, agreed by Coalition partners and then, if it involves legislation, there must be no fewer than 18 separate steps involving three separate legislatures. Talk about checks and balances. Only an alliance with Labour offered us the opportunity of progressing as a nation beyond this slow-motion politics.

But the truth is, that was not the only reason that an alliance with Labour came more naturally to us than the alternative. This is the truth that dare not speak its name. For while Labour and Plaid activists would often rub shoulders in the peace movement, the Miners' Strike and the Anti-Poll Tax protests of the 1980s – and of course, most fruitfully, during the Yes Campaign in 1997 – the only dialogue between the parties these days is the one around the Cabinet table. At all opportunities we try to maintain the pretence that the red-green Coalition is more a latter-day Molotov-Ribbentrop pact than an alliance of progressives, a temporary abeyance in hostilities between bitter enemies before normal service resumes.

The truth is more complicated. Nationalism and Labourism are the two great radical movements of twentieth-century Wales. Liberalism ceased to have deep social and cultural roots in Wales shortly after the Second World War. Conservatism is, by definition, an anti-radical anti-movement and a specifically Welsh personality for the party is a very recent phenomenon.

The Dragon has two tongues

The relationship, then, between Labour and Plaid Cymru remains the central narrative in Welsh politics. Although no-one should doubt the ferocity of the electoral rivalry, it cannot be characterised solely as one of outright opposition because it has also involved a process of interpellation, a calling-to-account. In this way Plaid has influenced Labour, drawing it in a nationalist direction. Meanwhile, Labour, through its unrivalled hegemony from the interwar period on, pushed Plaid towards its formal adoption of socialism as a philosophy in 1981.

The histories of the two movements, though superficially different, have followed the same trajectory from intellectual to popular movement, to party, and to government. In the case of British socialism, it took just under a hundred years from Robert Owen's first use of the term to Labour's first government in 1924. This puts Welsh nationalism's long wait for power – of 82 years – in some perspective.

What unites Welsh nationalism – at least in its home-grown version, as a liberation movement – and Welsh socialism is that they both are essentially expressions of a desire to transform Welsh society by challenging the existing relationships of political and economic power. While parties of the Right can often have a modernising programme, they cannot be described as radical or revolutionary in this deeper sense. Even in these politically promiscuous times, the terms 'radicals' and 'conservatives' are still the best words we have to describe the fundamental dividing line in politics: between those who want to confront entrenched power in a society and those who seek to defend it.

As parties of the Left, Labour and Plaid would be natural coalition allies, if it wasn't for the national question. Whereas even the mainstream of the Welsh Labour Party has come to accept Welsh nationhood as an objective reality, the degree of enthusiasm shown reflects a continuing ambiguity as regards the whole notion of national identity. For us the existence of nations is essential, as humanity can only develop its potential and its possibilities by developing them in different directions. Progressive internationalism is pluri-national by definition; and progressive nationalism is one of the greatest transformational forces in modern history. Labour sees nationalism as at best a diversion, at worst dangerously destructive. We, by contrast, are proud to belong to a philosophical tradition and an international political movement that can count among its ranks the likes of Tomáš Masaryk, Simón Bolívar, Mahatma Gandhi, Jomo Kenyatta, Michael Collins, and Thomas Jefferson.

But the ideological tension between Labour and nationalism has deeper roots than this familiar terrain. The Labour Party and Plaid Cymru represent two very different conceptions of what the Left in Wales should stand for. Welsh Labourism has remained rooted in a traditional and, in some senses, institutionally conservative social democracy. At its heart is a commitment to equality of outcome and opportunity to be achieved mainly through the redistribution of resources via the tax and benefits system to which New Labour, it has to be said, never fully signed up.

Welsh Labour's fidelity to Old Labour values – the 'clear red water' strategy articulated by Rhodri Morgan in a key speech in 2002 – is key to understanding both its relative resilience as a political force and its current crisis. While distancing itself from New Labour was strategically deft, the fact that the main levers of power relevant to the achievement of equality remain in the hands of a Whitehall Labour Government intent on the dismantling of the welfare state has left Labour in Wales demoralised and disorientated.

Far from presenting itself as a force for change, Welsh Labour has cast itself in the role of mounting a rearguard defence of social democracy in retreat. There is something self-limiting and ultimately self-defeating about this version of left-wing politics. Redistributive egalitarianism – the idea that the main purpose of a progressive government is to compensate for the inequalities thrown up by the market – sounds radical compared to the neo-liberal consensus of recent years. But the underlying assumption is intrinsically conservative: that the conditions and institutions which gave rise to the inequalities in the first place are unchallenged. As the world financial crisis continues to unfold around us, this position is politically unsustainable.

Plaid's alternative conception of what it means to be progressive is based around a much broader agenda of institutional change, including the democratisation of the market, the deepening of democracy itself, and the empowerment of the individual. Equality remains a prerequisite to the kind of humanised society and economy we want to create. This means preventing extremes of privilege and deprivation, and, in particular, preventing the hereditary transmission of advantage and disadvantage from determining the life chances of individuals. But equality is a means and not an end. The end is the enlargement of everyone's capacity to live a meaningful life.

These counterpoints to Labourism have always been there – from Saunders Lewis' distributist concept of *perchentyaeth* ('home ownership'), to D J Davies' advocacy of co-operative economics, Gwynfor Evans' emphasis on respect for the individual, and the formula of decentralist socialism arrived at by the Party in the early 1980s. Plaid's version of progressive politics is not so much about the socialisation of the economy, but its humanisation – including both the social and the personal dimensions of human life. Integral humanism – a phrase devised by the French Catholic thinker Jacques Maritain – perhaps comes closest to expressing Plaid's vision.

What unites all these elements is their emphasis on the need for a 'moral economy', not just the market economy so beloved of the free-market fundamentalists. The idea of a moral economy makes it clear that the economy does not exist outside of human moral questions of equality, dignity and respect for the environment; that the economy is not just a matter of supply and demand, but also right and wrong. Only through a moral economy can we provide holistically for human material and non-material needs, especially the need for a caring, nurturing, safe and human-scale environment.

Equality for us, then, has always been a means and not an end. The end is ensuring people have the opportunity to live big lives full of ambition, struggle, surprise, and success. The struggle to end extreme and entrenched inequalities of circumstance and opportunity – lifting people of out of poverty, sickness and drudgery – is a necessary step in the empowerment of ordinary men and women to achieve that larger life. But alongside the traditional social democratic notions of equality and community, we would also stress autonomy. This deep-seated human desire for independence – workers wanting to stand on their own two feet, nations wanting to go their own way – is the engine of innovation.

Gwynfor Evans, in his Foreword to Ioan Bowen Rees' *The Welsh Political Tradition*, (Plaid Cymru, 1975) summed up this aspect of Plaid's social thought in language reminiscent of the 'personalist' philosophy – the original *via media* between individualism and communitarianism favoured by both the last and current Pope – of Emmanuel Mounier and Nikolai Berdyaev:

> It begins from the premise that the supreme value on earth is that of the human person, whose humanity derives from his social nature. A humane social order will allow each person the fullest opportunity of achieving his or her potential. This requires close regard for material needs: but equally important are man's non-material needs, for the human person is mind and soul as well as body.

While these ideas run counter to the traditions of mainstream top-down, statist social democracy to which the Labour movement signed up from the 1930s, a dissident subcurrent has always percolated just beneath the surface: G D H Cole and the Guild Socialists, the Utopianism of the Co-operative movement, the syndicalism of *The Miners' Next Step* and the pluralism of the ILP. It is these left-libertarian elements within the Labour tradition, perhaps, that rendered a red-green alliance less incongruous than it might have appeared.

Transfiguring the actual, imagining the possible

In the political sphere, Plaid's key demand is self-government in the broadest possible sense. We are supposed to be a democratic society but most people are excluded from power, both in the sense of lacking influence over government but also in having very little control of their working lives or economic prospects. The central premise of humanism must be that people achieve a greater control over every aspect of their own lives. Welsh politics needs to become, in the words of Roberto Unger, the Harvard-based academic turned minister in Lula's Brazil, a "high-energy democracy".

Alongside the foot soldiers and the "trumpeters of the revolution", as Lenin once dubbed elected representatives, Plaid needs a new generation of 'organic intellectuals' to help ferment the signature policies that could embody the kind of transformation we want to see, illustrating our values and showing the voter where our head and our heart are as a party. Ignoring for one moment the practical limitations of the current constitutional settlement, what kind of policies might these be?

Well, as a modern echo of Saunders Lewis' distributism, in a genuinely humanist Wales each new Welsh citizen could be given at birth a form of social endowment – a basic stake in the wealth of society in the form of a guaranteed social inheritance. This could build on the Baby Bond established by the Westminster Government and the Child Bond which the One Wales Government has agreed to create from next year. This endowment should become a cashable resource on which an individual can draw at different points in their life – on going to university, on buying a house (drawing on our proposal of a first-time buyer's grant), getting married, having a first child, and so on. It could be increased for those from low-income families or those suffering some other disadvantage.

We could build on the revolutionary move to child-centred play-based learning through the Foundation Phase for three to seven year olds and replace the 'learning factory' approach to education and child development. We need to replace the Prussian model of rote learning adopted from 1870 onwards – which first tried to destroy our language and has been killing the natural creativity of generations of children ever since – with the kind of holistic and emancipatory vision of education developed by the Grundtvig schools in Denmark (which was such a strong influence on D J and Noëlle Davies), and the radical pedagogical ideas of R F Mackenzie, Paulo Freire, Ivan Illich and John Taylor Gatto. All of these place capacity above memory, skill above qualification, and the needs of the child above the needs of the economy.

Building on Ifan ab Owen Edwards' original vision for *Urdd Gobaith Cymru* we could also create a National Youth Service offering year-long postings on leaving school to all 16–18 year olds, who would in return receive a top-up to their Child Bond. This could be modelled on the highly successful Canadian *Katimavik* programme launched in 1977. *Katimavik* – an Inuit word meaning the place where, at the end of a hunt, people would gather to share their catch and swap stories – comprises service teams of twelve young people, half of them male and half female, who, supervised by adults, undertake a series of three-month projects in different parts of Canada. During their time on the programme, the young people live, work, eat, cook and clean together, developing social skills as well as a sense of personal responsibility.

With the public sector playing such a dominant role in our society and economy, it cannot and should not be immune from the transformation we seek. Welsh citizens, all of whom pay tax in one form or another, have a right to demand that public services funded by their taxes continually improve. The idea of standardised services provided by a centralised bureaucracy belongs to the last century. The only alternative offered to this model of state provision so far has been privatisation. But profit-making businesses are not the only option. We should be encouraging experimentation with new forms of not-for-profit, mutual and community-owned providers of public services.

Industrial democracy was one of the main themes of the Party in the 1970s. In the wake of the collapse of neo-liberalism, it is an idea that has contemporary relevance as we seek a new model of economic governance. An attractive alternative to both the unfettered market and state ownership is the Meidner Plan, developed in Sweden in the 1970s, though never implemented. According to the plan, companies with more than 100 employees would have to transfer a portion of their profits (10%–30%) in the form of newly issued stock to employee-owned investment funds administered by the trade unions. The cash from the profit would remain within the firm, available as equity capital for investment. The voting rights of the shares would go to employee representatives. Over time the employees would own an ever-greater share of the company.

Alternatively, we could create a National Solidarity Fund, modelled on the Québec Solidarity Fund started in 1983. These worker-led venture capital funds now represent more than one third of venture capital in Canada. Established through tax credits to firms and some public seed capital, the funds channel the savings of Canadian workers into small and medium-sized companies. The funds are independently managed, aiming to ensure high returns and diversified risks. Studies have suggested that the value of the tax incentives – worth up to 40% of the funds invested – is paid back to the Government in about three years because of the increase in payroll taxes through jobs created and the reduction in welfare payments.

We also need to find new ways of encouraging the creation and development of new businesses. One proven way of doing this is to reduce business taxes. The socialist case in favour of corporate taxation is a weak one, as redistribution can be achieved much more effectively through progressive income and capital gains tax. Business taxes result in lower levels of investment. The *Journal of Public Economics'* 2005 review of international practice over three decades has pointed to evidence that a reduction in corporate taxes of 10% increases economic growth by 2%. While we don't currently have the ability to vary corporation taxes, we do have the power to vary business rates. I would like to see a Plaid-led government announce that it was going to cut the business rate by 25% a year over four years, cutting it in effect to zero by the end of the term. This would massively reduce the start-up and running costs for existing businesses and would give an immediate stimulus for the economy. It will, of course, require savings in the economic development budget and it will take time to work. But work it will.

The transformation of the economy is, of course, the central question in Welsh life. Without improving our economic position we cannot achieve the kind of social, cultural and environmental changes we want to see. In one sense, without independence, no Welsh government can succeed economically. In relative terms, we can only fail better. As a Cambridge study recently discussed in the *Western Mail* (29 August, 2008) demonstrated, we will always be at a relative economic disadvantage within the UK because the prioritisation of the City of London and the south-east of England sucks in labour and investment and crowds out economic investment.

The principal task of a nationalist economic policy has to be to close the wealth gap to such an extent that independence becomes a politically feasible option for a majority of the population. That requires the achievement of sufficient autonomy over taxation and borrowing, industrial policy and financial regulation that we are able to influence the underlying determinants of economic performance. This should be seen not so much as a halfway house, but as the construction of the bridge to the future. Many will want to go with us only part of the way at the outset. However, if the foundations can be shown to be solid, there is no reason why the people of Wales should not choose to complete their historic journey.

The politics of renewal, the renewal of politics

Of course, it is not just policy that must change if we are to create the new society, but politics itself. Here I think the Days of May to July 2007 contain important lessons.

The first insight is that we do still need strong political

parties with deep roots in society and well-defined political programmes. Anti-politics – the politics of protest pure and simple – is ultimately incapable of bringing about the national economic and social transformation we desire.

Like most political parties today, Plaid Cymru lacks two ingredients essential to a healthy political party: mass membership and a cadre class of intellectuals. The former has been a perennial problem. The Party has to rediscover some of its evangelical zeal and send its best orators out on the road again to win hearts and minds to the cause. As to the latter, as Elfyn Llwyd recently commented, the Party that was once top-heavy with PhDs and pamphlets has simply stopped publishing anything of note – with the exception of the ubiquitous blogs and press releases. This has to change. The Party needs to find a publisher or else become its own. It needs an e-journal on the lines of the Huffington Post. And it needs its own arm's-length think tank, along the lines of the Bevan Foundation.

The second major insight is that there needs to be a strong prospect of political change. One party in power in perpetuity is corrosive of public trust and interest in democracy. For progressives, democracy has to be about the creation of the new. This is how we make material progress; this is how we challenge vested interests and outdated practices; this is how each new generation gets the opportunity to express its new ideas and insights and turn them into their new reality. Change is the lifeblood of democracy and the motor of human progress.

Thirdly, political pluralism – a product of our partially proportional electoral system – is good for democracy because it requires the agreement of a political programme. While a manifesto is conceived primarily as a platform for the election – essentially a political marketing brochure – a coalition programme is a much more detailed and comprehensive statement of the political direction and commitments of a government. Because of the carefully and very publicly mediated nature of its founding statement, a Coalition government is arguably more accountable as a consequence. In place of the rather episodic nature of modern government – consisting of legislation, budgets, reaction to events and the endless round of headline-chasing – coalitions at least have an explicit medium-term political and societal strategy and are much more robust as a result.

But coalitions are not without their potential pitfalls or problems. There is an ever-present danger that through interminable coalition discussions, politics becomes diluted into a succession of each party's second-best solutions as the more radical policies to which one or other party object are simply left out of the final draft. Coalition politics could thus become a recipe for inertia because of the need to sustain fragile deals between parties and the need to uphold unity within each of the parties in the alliances.

There is also the danger that government becomes as much the outcome of negotiations as of elections and thus becomes 'captured' by the political class. In particular, closed regional lists give a privileged role to the party machine as the gatekeepers of power. With party membership in Wales in total standing at less than 30,000, this means that 99.9% of the population are excluded from a key stage in the democratic process through what the Italians call *partitocrazia* – the party bureaucrats and power brokers that wield authority with no public accountability at all.

There are three procedural solutions to these problems:

1 We could combine representative democracy with direct democracy. The Welsh Assembly was created by a referendum, and there is no reason why plebiscitary referenda could not become a normal element of the Welsh political scene. Far from undermining representative democracy, direct democracy actually enriches it. There are a number of free-vote issues, for example the question of presumed consent and organ donation, where the people

are at least as well qualified as the politicians to decide the outcome to a debate. Holding regular plebiscitary referenda – to coincide with elections – will have an invigorating effect on the public's sense of ownership over democratic politics. In particular, if the parties disagree about the inclusion of an item in a programme, rather than simply leaving it out, it should be the subject of a plebiscite. This has two advantages. It ensures that the programme doesn't simply become the lowest common denominator of the party programmes, the non-controversial ideas with which everyone agrees. It also gives a central role to the people in key areas of political dispute.

2 We need to create a 'Party Forum' – larger and more representative than my Party's National Executive Committee but smaller than the National Council (in our case) that ratified the original agreement, to scrutinise and hold ministers to account on delivery. It is vital to the health of democracy – not to speak of the political fortunes of any Coalition party – that a programme, once signed up to, is actually delivered. This is much more likely if the political base is kept fully informed of progress and fully involved in any debate on the correct interpretation of a programme commitment (for us, the case of the proposed Welsh-language daily newspaper *Y Byd* was a salutary lesson). A party has to carry its activists and core supporters with it on its political journey, or the journey will be a lot shorter than anticipated. This Forum should have the right to recall a Special Conference to consider pulling out of a coalition, a possibility which should concentrate the minds of the party's own ministers as well as those of our Coalition partners.

3 Thirdly, we need to find a way of bringing all the social movements – not just the trade unions – into the work of political parties. The government of Lula in Brazil has been very adept at maintaining a constant and direct dialogue with the social movements that supported his presidential

bid. Plaid has begun experimenting with Contact Group meetings with leading organisations in the language and environmental movements. This needs to be broadened to other sectors and formalised through observer status, with speaking rights for social movement representatives. Internally, there is a case for the creation of new party sections that could, in turn, be represented at meetings of the Party Forum.

The necessity of change

The innovations outlined above seek to resolve differences between Coalition partners. They help by involving party members and the electorate more closely in the work of the Government. This will not make for 'stable government'. Yet politics needs levers of destablilisation to open up the possibility of change and to challenge vested interests and entrenched political power. The politics of 'safety first' – a slogan in the Great Depression – is the last thing we need when our economy and society are crying out for transformation.

Admittedly, the need for 'stable government' was one of the reasons given by my Party's leadership for the ultimate choice of Labour as a coalition partner in the summer of 2007. Labour ministers, too, have confided in me their belief that this is the first time, since devolution, that Wales has had a genuinely stable government in the sense of a rock-solid majority and shared political values. In turn, these have enabled the administration to plan its policies with a greater degree of political certainty.

Societies – even those undergoing radical social and economic transformation – do sometimes need periods of political stability in order to enact the transformation. In other words, radical politics must run both hot and cold. Nevertheless, political inertia is probably a far greater threat to progress than any amount of instability. As the science-fiction visionary Philip K Dick said once, with characteristic acuity:

> Do not assume that order and stability are always good in a society
> or in a universe. The old, the ossified, must always give way to new
> life, and the birth of new things. Before new things can happen,
> the old must perish.

Does this mean that Wales, like most other democracies, should oscillate between left and right? As a radical, I would welcome that about as much as the prospect of time running backwards. For me, one of the more telling arguments in favour of devolution – and indeed, independence – is the banishment of the prospect of a right-wing government ever running Wales again, at least in its entirety. On a more positive note, many of Plaid's ablest propagandists – especially Phil Williams – held out the prospect of a self-governing Wales emulating the social achievements of Scandinavia, where in Sweden, for example, social democracy reigned unchallenged for two generations.

The problem is that eventually a one-party state will morph into some version of dystopia. This is part of what Hegel called the "contradictions of progress". When they come to be put into practice through the exercise of political power, radical or revolutionary ideas become bureaucratic and institutionalised. In other words, they degenerate into their own form of conservatism. As someone who was shouted down as a bolshy youngster by the massed ranks of the Valleys' *nomenklatura*, I know how true this is.

Conservatives can sometimes modernise societies that have become stuck, as genuine radicalism has decayed into something of a spent force. But, as we saw during the 'Thatcher revolution', the consequences of this kind of modernisation are often fairly brutal. In Wales we are fortunate that the political challenge to Labourism's power base comes from a competing movement of the Left. The question for the Labour Party is whether it can renew itself in power as a radical, transformational movement. After a decade of total power and a century of cultural hegemony this will be enormously difficult. The question for Plaid is not whether to challenge Labour for dominance, but when.

Of course, a coalition as unexpected as that between Labour and Plaid has itself had an enlivening effect on Welsh politics. However, when grand coalitions become semi-permanent fixtures of the political scene, as they have been in Austria for most of the post-war period, in order simply to keep other parties out of power, then perhaps they become a historic compromise too far.

Who Do We Represent?

Like the party system itself, societies contain radical and conservative elements. In this sense a political party that literally seeks to represent everyone ends up representing no-one. Every party needs an electoral base in the sense of a core constituency whose interests and aspirations it can authentically claim to represent. By definition, Labour's popular base for over a century has been organised labour, while Plaid's bedrock of support has been among so-called Welsh-identifiers, particularly Welsh speakers.

But the success of a political party is determined by its ability to turn its base into the foundation for a much broader social alliance. For much of the twentieth century, Labour enjoyed a position of overarching political hegemony encompassing most sections of Welsh culture and society. Plaid has achieved something similar – but only within the confines of Welsh-speaking society.

It is probably no accident that Plaid Cymru is probably the last mainland, mainstream political party in the UK to invest in geo-demographic software – the kind of database that allows you to target segments of the electorate according to their socio-economic characteristics. In part, this represents a historic failure by the nationalist movement to move beyond an ethno-linguistic political identification to embrace a socio-economic approach relevant across Wales.

Labour has had its own very different problems with class. Old Labour saw itself primarily as representing trade union-organised workers by default rather than by design, mostly male, mostly in industrial occupations. New Labour attempted to reach out to the middle classes with a much broader emphasis, beyond the world of work, on 'quality of life'. Both these paths are unacceptable. The first is too narrow to be genuinely transformative. The second, if not exactly excluding the poor and the under-privileged, takes their support as a political given.

In the twenty-first century, political hegemony is up for grabs. This is partly because part of the traditional working class vote has detached itself from Labour due to disappointment with Blair and Brown. But by far the bigger problem is the fact that the traditional working class no longer forms the clear, coherent majority it did in the days of heavy industry. New social groups and new social movements have emerged whose interests are only weakly articulated by the political system. This represents a profound political opportunity for Plaid to break out of its traditional heartland to become a truly pan-Wales party.

So what kind of new social alliance could Plaid knit together that would be capable of winning majoritarian support? Plaid must continue its work of the last thirty years to poach or unpick traditional working-class support from Labour. We need to continue to convince those who depend on the public sector for their wage or their benefit that political change need not be a threat to them, but an opportunity. But old loyalties die hard, and if we are to build a new dynamic, we need to look to new social formations that have less to lose and more to gain from a change of direction; groups that are not defending long-established vested interests but have aspirations for themselves and their families which can be fashioned into a political programme for society.

14

Changing the course of a nation

Plaid Cymru Spring Conference, Newport – 2008

THERE COMES A time once in every generation when there is an opportunity to change the course of a nation. We are living in that time. We were born into a stateless, powerless, all too often leaderless nation dominated by a larger neighbour whose political values are so clearly different from our own. Our history is littered with regrets, with setbacks and disappointments and stories of what might have been. But even in those moments of defeat, there has remained the one constant in our history as a nation, and that is our hope that tomorrow's generation will see a future that is better than our past. It is that hope that has sustained us as a nation. It's that hope that brought everyone in this room into the politics of this Party. And it's that hope we renew here every year at Conference.

There are people watching this at home, and even maybe one or two in the hall, who have not yet joined our movement – people of other parties or no party, people who were once members but the passion that they had somehow dimmed.

My message to you today is simple: even if you hate politics – or even *because* you hate what passes for politics in 2008 – if you love Wales, your place is here. Standing side by side with me. With every woman, man and child in this hall and this movement. Because a nation such as ours can only move forward if we march together. So join us. Add your voice to ours. Don't just wish for the change. Don't just be a witness of the change. Be the agent of the change that you want to see.

And there really has never been a better moment to join this movement for democracy and progress that we call the Party of Wales. Because on this day, in this hour, in this moment in our history, we are poised on the cusp of the greatest change that any nation on this earth can ever see at any point in its history. And that is to assume the mantle of responsibility for charting our own future.

For the first time in the entire history of our nation, we have ministers in our own Government whose only loyalty is to the people of Wales – who pay no loyalty and owe no allegiance to any overlord in London. No government will be perfect – not even our own. I was brought up a Calvinist and had the doctrine of original sin inculcated into me as a child, so I know that imperfection is an inescapable fact of the human condition – and that is as true of political parties as much as individuals. We won't always get it right. But there is one significant difference now, and that is that the mistakes that we make are our own. We can measure the actions of our Government, *our Government,* against our ideals and our values. That is a momentous change, because it contains within it the seed of possibility: that we finally might begin to build the better tomorrow for which we've so long yearned.

The doubters and the detractors and the latter-day League of Empire Loyalists will continue to say that this nation of ours can never be free, that Wales will never take its place among the other 193 free nations of the world. Well, to coin a political phrase, I say Yes We Can. Yes We Can be a successful nation like any other on this Earth – not more successful, maybe, but certainly no less. In the words of Parnell, imprinted on the SNP's White Paper on Scotland's Future: "No man has the right to fix the boundary to the march of a nation."

Those in the London parties who oppose independence because it would rid them of their power base, of their prestige, of their patronage, are already too late. Because we have in Wales a new generation, taught for the first time about *their* history – not the history of kings and queens – taught their national language, taught to have pride in themselves and in their limitless potential. They are already independent, in mind as well as spirit, and they are at last showing to the world the self-confidence that at times we have lacked. This is not the Welsh Not, Wales Cannot generation. This is the Wales Can, Yes, We Can generation.

The energy and passion in the New Wales is there for everyone to see, from Millennium Centre to Millennium Stadium. In this new millennium, history won't be something that is done to us. It will be history that we will make ourselves. We will teach every new generation the most important lesson of all: that their Wales and their world is theirs to shape as much as any nation.

We are at the moment a nation brimming with energy, from Bryn to Duffy to the Grand Slam to the Swans in the Championship and – dare I mention in Newport – Cardiff City. It's like someone has taken the stopper out of a country that has been hemmed in for years and is at last beginning to breathe.

Ac i garu'ch cymydog mae'n rhaid i chi yn gyntaf ddysgu i garu chi eich hun...
('And to love your neighbour, you must first learn to love yourselves')

We are a nation of performers, because it's through performance that we express who we are. Historically the chapel became a place of sanctuary for us because, at a time when many of our ancestors – including the Gwenhwyseg speakers of Monmouthshire – were not allowed to utter one word of Welsh in a public realm that didn't recognise the validity of their existence (even though for many of them it was the only language that they ever knew), in the pulpit and in the pew they found a place where they could address each other and their God in their own words. And through faith, and through prayer and through studying their Bible – *their* Bible – they learned that their language or culture was worthy of the same respect as any other and that to love your neighbour, you first have to learn to love yourself.

And that other great arena where we have expressed our identity is the sporting field, because that was the one place where our nationhood was not denied but celebrated. Where 15 men in red could compete on equal terms with any other national team. Few among us can imagine what it could be like to wear that jersey on that field while an entire nation pours out its emotion. But there is one man on this stage who does, and that's Roger Bidgood, who was capped for Wales five times in the 1990s. Roger played for Wales five years after he was originally picked because the weather intervened – now, that's the kind of persistence that we need in this Party, and Roger, I know that you will show the same commitment to Wales in the chamber of Caerphilly Borough as you showed on the rugby field for Newport, Caerphilly and Wales.

Roger will know from personal experience the power of the 16th man: the nation willing on the nation. It's that self-belief we have to awaken in this country of ours.

We need to lift the ceiling on our ambition as a nation. Let's not raise false expectations that we are going to be able to do that overnight, because the legacy with which we've been left is a heavy one. This nation was crucified in the twentieth century through naked greed on a cross of gold. King Coal may have gone, but the shadow of that crown of thorns is still all too visible in so many of our communities. Those scars are there not just in the landscape and in the lungs of our people, they are also embedded deep in our collective memory. This country could have been the richest in the world. They mined every ore, every mineral imaginable in Wales: not just coal, but iron ore, slate, limestone, copper, zinc, lead, silver and gold. The only thing we didn't have was diamonds, but there's enough coal left in the ground so give us a couple of million years and eventually we'll have them too.

The tragedy of modern Wales is that apart from a few square miles of amazing architecture in the centre of Cardiff, we as a people never profited from our own vast wealth. They left us with a legacy but robbed us of our inheritance. And while the Wales of today is in so many ways different from the Wales of a century ago, there are continuities. We are still a net exporter of two things, energy and people.

In the Thirties it was coal and the unemployed; today it's gas, electricity and graduates. We're still poorer and sicker than our neighbour. But the most pernicious legacy is this belief that remains buried in our subconscious minds that somehow we are predetermined to poverty, that relative failure is our fate, that we will never stand tall. That's the lie peddled by our opponents. That's the mountain of self-doubt that we have to conquer.

And just as mountains are not climbed in one stride, it is the small steps, the little victories in every county, in every corner of this country – every vote we win, every seat we hold, every community we represent, every council we run – that take us one small step further on the path to self-confidence and the road to self-government. Each local campaign is a building block in the New Wales we will create tomorrow.

Because that's the wager we make with the people of Wales: if we can demonstrate our competence and our commitment, then we can prove to them that this nation no longer needs to outsource and offshore its democracy and its economy to London. We can do it ourselves and we can do it better.

And it's fitting that we should be here in Newport, where the idea of a democratic government answerable to the people of Wales was first mooted in modern times, in the Great Newport Rising. Henry Vincent, the Chartist leader, whose arrest for speeches was the catalyst for the events of 1839, said this in the spring of that year on his tour of the Gwent Valleys:

> I showed the people how they would be bettered in circumstances were they possessed of law-making powers... Wales would make an excellent Republic.

The Chartists marched under the colours of our flag – red for the people, green for the land and white as symbol of peace. Let this banner then be the symbol of the Welsh democracy we are pledged to create. Let it remind us of a rendezvous with history that we in this generation are determined to keep.

And when you are delivering leaflets in the wind and the rain, remember those that that gave their lives for our Welsh democracy. Remember the spirit of nineteen-year-old George Shell, a carpenter from Pontypool involved in the Newport Rising. Left to bleed to death, he had written these words to his parents the night before:

> I shall this night be engaged in a struggle for freedom and should it please God to spare my life, I shall see you soon; but if not, grieve not for me, I shall fall in a noble cause.

And fighting for the liberty and the dignity of the people and the land that you love is the noblest cause of all. In Newport then, in Lhasa today, bullets may kill a marcher, but they cannot kill the forward march of a nation. We will build that Welsh democracy – even if we have to dig down deep into the bedrock of our soul. We owe it to those who lost their lives outside the Westgate.

But more importantly we owe it to all the generations to come to finally realise our dream of a future that will be better than our past.

15

Labour is now
Robin Hood in reverse

Plaid Cymru Autumn Conference,
Aberystwyth – 2008

CEREDIGION IS ONE of the great cradles of Welsh dissent. Sometimes I wish I had the gumption of Lewis Pryse MP, who in the seventeenth century refused to swear the oath of allegiance to George I following the Jacobite rebellion. He is still the only Welsh MP to be expelled permanently from the House of Commons since the Restoration.

David Ivon Jones was born here and T E Nicholas – Niclas y Glais – died here. And the evergreen Cynog Dafis is very much alive here, and keeping us all on our intellectual toes.

Next year is the 400th anniversary of one of Ceredigion's most lauded sons: the poet, genealogist, thief and JP – now that's an impressive CV – Thomas Jones, of course; better known as the Welsh Robin Hood, Twm Siôn Cati. Born in a time of great upheaval, of poverty and injustice, he became a highwayman first to prise his own mother out of poverty but later to carry out his own primitive version of what we today would recognise as a redistributive fiscal policy. In other words, he robbed from the rich to give to the poor.

The general conditions of life now could not be more different from Wales in the reign of Henry VIII. But in one important sense, Twm would recognise in today's Kingdom two of the perennial barriers to progress: greed and hypocrisy.

The Tudors were meant to liberate us – we had put *y Mab Darogan* ('the Son of Prophecy') back on the English throne to vanquish the Norman Oppressor. But they soon forgot our loyalty and banned our language and what was then our religion, to build up an empire and enrich themselves and their courtiers.

Labour too was meant to liberate us. But yet again the loyalty of the ordinary people of Wales has been rewarded with betrayal. This Government, which was meant to be the antidote to the selfishness of the Thatcher years, has ended up with the obscene spectacle of a Labour Prime Minister, Gordon Brown, once held up as the one remaining hope during the bitter years of disappointment under Blair, inviting Mrs Thatcher to tea and cakes at No. 10 to emphasise the underlying continuity of economic orthodoxy. Is it any wonder that Labour has lost half of its members and trade unions are disaffiliating in droves? For these last eleven years this Labour Government has been Robin Hood in reverse, heaping taxes on the poor, while handing out peerages and tax breaks to their supporters among the super-rich.

In politics, in history, each decade has a defining issue, each new generation a challenge that has to be overcome if their society is to move forward. The issue, the challenge for us could not be clearer: it is the fundamental unfairness at the heart of our economy and our society. Let's remind ourselves of the scale of inequality we're talking about: the ratio of the FTSE 100 Chief Executives' pay to the average wage has gone from 10 to 1 in 1979 to 100 to 1 in 2006. That is to say, the typical Chief Executive makes more by the middle of one single working week than an average worker makes in a year.

Gordon Brown recognised Labour's failure on social justice for the first time last week. But where was Gordon Brown when Peter Mandelson, co-architect of New Labour, made his infamous remark about Labour being relaxed about people getting filthy rich. Labour bought into the nostrums of neo-liberalism: that a rising tide lifts all boats – that as long as everyone is getting richer, it doesn't matter if some are getting richer than others. Well, now we know if you follow that path, you end up with a society of have-nots and have-yachts.

The United Kingdom – after the USA – is now officially the most unequal country in the industrialised world. And this inequality expresses itself through geography too, as we learned last month that the gap between Wales and the south-east of England is greater now than any time in the last 60 years. The economic success of London is the cause of our relative failure, according to economists at Cambridge University. The south-east has crowded out growth in the rest of the UK by constantly sucking in labour and investment from elsewhere.

All of this hasn't happened by accident. It's a direct result of Government policy: the neglect of manufacturing and the pandering to the City, Crossrail, the Olympics and a million new homes for the south-east. And Gordon Brown has been at the forefront of the policies. The so-called socialist son of the manse who has presided over the most generous ever tax breaks to the already-wealthy and the biggest extension of means testing for the poor since the 1930s.

In the panic mini-budget designed to quell growing anger among the low-paid about the abolition of the 10p tax rate, what we had from the Government was a stop-gap measure, using money borrowed from the City, only available for a year and still leaving a million people not fully compensated. Compare that to Labour raising the inheritance tax threshold from £300k to £600k, and then to £700k after 2010: a gift of £1.6 billion to the richest 6% of families. Then there's capital gains tax, slashed from 40% to 18% at a time when governments in

Germany and the Netherlands, led by parties of the right, have just introduced a levy on excessive executive bonuses.

Our Fairness Commission will look at all these issues. But I for one do agree with the TUC that we need new higher tax rates for the elite of very high earners so we can spread the burden more fairly. Let's have people on £100,000 paying 50%. And, surely, the top 1% who earn over £220,000 a year can afford to pay even more. That should enable us to take those earning under £10,000 out of tax altogether. And let's look at the annual wealth taxes levied on the super-rich in Austria, Belgium, France, Germany, Norway, the Netherlands, Sweden, Spain and Switzerland. If they can do it, why can't we? Because the Labour Party has been bought. Bought by the very vested interests in the City and among the super-rich that it was founded to challenge and to counter.

Inequality matters. It is the root of so many of our problems. It creates a society where there is super-abundance for the few, anxiety for the many – and for the people at the very bottom, poverty, drudgery and disease. The modern consumerist society thrives on inequality because it's the engine of envy, of limitless desire that is never ever quite fulfilled because there is always someone else with more than you – that is the motor of the capitalist economy. It's this orgy of consumption in an unequal society on both sides of the Atlantic that has driven people to rack up huge household debt. In turn, that has led us to the financial and economic meltdown we are now facing.

Advertising invites us all to conclude that the measure of our lives is not the quality of our relationships but the quantity of our possessions, not the content of our hearts but the contents of our wallets. So when the good times rolled, people were given the hard sell of cheap credit. That's why personal debt in the UK has soared to £1.4 trillion. We have not just mortgaged our houses, we've mortgaged our futures. We've mortgaged our lives. It's the repayments on this debt that created the market in debt securities that have been generating the huge City bonuses. And it's the sub-prime version of this – the selling of debt to those who can't afford it – that now threatens the very future of the financial system.

Now the music and the merry-go-round has stopped, we are all in for a rough ride. The people who can least afford it will bear the most pain. But people even on middle incomes are worried by debt, the fall in house prices, recession, what's going to happen to their pensions, the growing cost of care. Add to that global warming, peak oil and escalating food and fuel costs and you see why people are beginning to call this the Age of Insecurity.

There are many things that worry me about the Conservative Party – but what particularly worries me is whether a man whose first leader's speech to the Conservative Party Conference ended with the words "Let sunshine win the day" has quite understood the mood of the moment. Even more disconcertingly, Cameron let slip that he was a fan of *Gavin and Stacey*. He's even taken to speaking in a Welsh accent and says he's looking forward to a 'tidy' result in Wales at the next election.

Let's think about this for a second. Nessa is a single mother who got pregnant through a one night stand. Stacey lives with her unemployed mother and her sexually-confused uncle Bryn, also unemployed. I don't mean to be funny but I'm having a spot of bother reconciling this slightly dysfunctional but no-less-lovable-for-it slice of Barry life with the man who said:

> I'm going to be as radical a social reformer as Mrs Thatcher was an economic reformer… dealing with the issues of family breakdown, welfare dependency… and the problems that we see in too many of our communities.

Cameron says he loves Smithy. Smithy, of course, is the absent father and – how can we put it gently? – he has probably never tried the Atkins diet. And yet Cameron, who thinks Smithy is "great", attacks black fathers for abandoning their children and says fat people are to blame for their own obesity. So is Cameron saying it's OK to be a fat absent father if you're white and from Essex, or just if you're his favourite comedy character?

No, that's not really what's occurring, is it, David – or should I call you Dai? What you're trying to do is fool millions into thinking that you're in touch with their lives and with their values when actually you're so far removed that not even Bryn's sat-nav could find you. So if you were hoping for a guest appearance in *Gavin & Stacey*, forget it; they're going to have Duffy instead. Never mind, though – I hear they're doing a Christmas remake of *To The Manor Born*. More your style.

Let's have no illusions about where the Conservatives stand on equality. Between 1980 and 2000 the number of children in poverty rose from 1.4 million to 4.4 million. So when the Conservatives talk about the broken society, they're right – and they should know: they broke it. In Britain today, one in six adults are suffering from depression. Stress, anxiety and depression are responsible for a third of days lost at work. Alcohol-related illness and death are on the increase because people are seeking temporary relief from the stresses and strains of their daily insecurities. This isn't because people are failing to take responsibility for themselves. It's because we made a God out of the Market, and that God has failed us.

On both sides of the Atlantic the economic model of neo-liberalism is broken and people are crying out for new political leadership. There is some irony that New Labour should find itself forced by circumstances to realise one of the long-cherished dreams of the Old Left and – in taking Northern Rock into public ownership – begin to nationalise the banks. And over in the States, a Republican Party that had long railed against the dangers of government intervention last week brought about the greatest nationalisation in human history.

Is this the worst economic situation since the 1930s? Alistair Darling seems to think so. And the worst Labour Government? There's certainly an air of the Ramsay MacDonald about

Gordon Brown: uncomfortable on camera, ineffectual, a political contortionist once described by Winston Churchill as the Boneless Wonder. If you wonder why the shadows under Gordon Brown's eyes are so dark – it's the spectre of 1931 staring him in the face.

The great lesson of the 1930s was the utter bankruptcy of the free-market model, which leads to excessive speculation driven by greed and an over-mighty financial sector. By the 1980s we had forgotten that lesson and so we got two decades of privatisation and the deregulation of financial services. So here we go again. This crisis did not come out of thin air. It wasn't like some comet suddenly striking the earth. This was the direct result of right-wing neo-liberal market ideology and the political power of the City over the economy.

A bolder leader than Brown – one more sure of themselves – would rip up the rule book. As well as reintroducing a progressive tax system and a windfall tax on energy companies, we could do what the US Treasury has done and offer a guarantee to mortgage companies on properties where they were prepared to accept a 15% write-off of the property price below the current market rate. This would keep people in their homes and avoid repossession – and mean people could have a new, affordable mortgage at a fixed rate.

We could buy appropriate unsold properties and turn them into badly needed social housing. We could give people a greater sense of control over their working lives by putting industrial democracy back on the agenda and implementing the Swedish Meidner Plan, requiring companies to give a proportion of their shares every year to their own employees. In the short term, we could reintroduce the retail price controls on electricity and gas removed by Ofgem in 2002. In the long term, we could move away from the broken privatised utility model and create a Glas Cymru for the Welsh energy supply companies. We could also bring the railways in Wales into public ownership as soon as the current franchise ends.

The most serious financial crisis since the Depression should be an opportunity for the Left and a crisis for the Right. But the distinction between left and right in British politics was abolished a long time ago, when Gordon Brown sold his soul. All that's left now is personality politics, and Gordon Brown doesn't have one. So that leaves our comrades in the Welsh Labour Party with a choice. Either they strap themselves to the decks of a party and a government that has failed, or they strike out anew by themselves. A truly Welsh, independent Labour Party could survive the coming *Götterdämmerung*. But that will mean breaking their umbilical chord with London.

There are those über-unionist fanatics who would rather commit political suicide with Gordon Brown in some Whitehall bunker than try and fight for a future for progressive politics in Wales. But the days in which Welsh men and women paid fealty to overlords in London are coming to an end. The message to Welsh Labour is clear: liberate yourself, or the people of Wales will liberate themselves from you.

Because for all our economic problems, this is a country that is self-confident as never before. 2008 has been the year of the dragon. From the Grand Slam to Calzaghe, the greatest haul ever of Welsh Olympic medals to Only Men Aloud and the Ysgol Glanaethwy choir, to the first ever Welsh winners of Big Brother and Mr Gay UK, to Lyn Evans, who yesterday switched on the biggest scientific experiment ever. We are a modern nation brimming with talent and diversity.

There are difficult times ahead. But the days in which we looked to others for our salvation are coming to a close. Of course, if our hands were on the levers of power, would we be cowering at the feet of foreign utility companies who charge us more in Wales than in England and more again than in France? No, we wouldn't have privatised them in the first place. Would we allow Chief Executives to pay less in tax as a proportion of their income than those who clean their offices? No, because that kind of energy saps the determination of people to improve their lives.

We don't have all the tools we need to build the new Wales we want. But we do at least have in our own Government, forged through our own democracy, a shield. Who will hold that shield when the current First Minister leaves the battlefield? We have our own answer to that question, but Labour is at a loss. There has even been talk of a knight in somewhat tarnished armour, riding to the rescue of the poor befuddled masses of the Welsh Labour Party. You've guessed it: Peter Hain. I would have thought that having been Alun Michael's campaign manager would disqualify you permanently for the job. Word of advice, Peter: don't go offering Gwenda a peerage, please. Remember Blaenau Gwent. Elfyn will say you did; you'll say no, you didn't; and most people will end up believing Elfyn.

But another more serious point. The days when politicians can take people for granted are gone. In Westminster we represent the same valley, the valley that I'm from. But we represent two very different versions of the future of Wales. If you in your hubris really think you can lead this country when you don't even believe we're ready for a Parliament – when you trumpeted the goals of social justice in pamphlet after pamphlet, but sat on your hands in Cabinet meetings again and again – then call that by-election and I'll see you on the streets of Gwaun-Cae-Gurwen and let the people decide the nation they want to be.

16

We must own our own mistakes and our own solutions

Plaid Cymru Spring Conference, Cardiff – 2009

AT THIS SPRING Conference if there is one single message we must communicate in the weeks that are left to the European elections, the largest democratic election on the face of the planet after the subcontinent of India, then it is this: the world is changing – rapidly, relentlessly, irrevocably – and we in Wales have no choice but to change with it. The only question is whether we have the courage and the confidence as a nation and a people to begin to make those changes on our own terms. Are we content, as humanity faces the great challenges of the twenty-first century, for Wales to be stuck in the sidelines, in the slipstream of history, or are we determined to chart our own course through the waters we face ahead? In the next few years we must decide what kind of a nation we want to be, and the choice that we make will affect all of our lives. We have no choice but to choose. In life and in the history of our nation, an abstention is itself a choice – a refusal to accept responsibility for our own future. At this time that is a choice that we can ill afford to make.

It was the Breton philosopher Ernest Renan who answered his own question – 'What is a nation?' – by saying it was a daily referendum (*un plébiscite de tous les jours*) on whether to continue to be a nation. It was while writing *When Was Wales* in the shadow of 1979 that the late great Gwyn Alf Williams came up with a similar formulation, when he said that Wales exists only if we choose it, and that it is up to each generation to make that choice. This generation is ready to make that choice and our question is not when Wales was but when our Wales will be.

There will always be those content to see us continually at the mercy of decisions that others make on our behalf, to see us buffeted by storms of others' making. I am fed up of seeing my country on the receiving end of other people's bad decisions. An independent Wales will be no Utopia – damn it, I think I've written the headline for Monday's *Western Mail* – but here's the crucial difference: we will own our own mistakes and our own solutions. There is nothing more empowering than being the author of your own destiny, and that is what we want this nation and each and every one of its citizens to be.

There is nothing about that statement that is insular, or parochial, or backward-looking, or any of the various epithets that our opponents over the years have thrown at us. And as a man who is proud to count a daughter of Worcester as his mother, there is nothing anti-English about it either. The simple truth is, as the troubled histories of empires – small or large – down the ages show, no country ever ruled another well.

There is no better proof of that axiom than the current economic difficulties. This is a global crisis but it is having a very different effect depending on where you live. London is the only part of the UK where unemployment has actually fallen – down 33,000 compared to a year ago, while we in Wales have seen a rise of 28,000.

There is one very simple reason for this. The policies of the UK Government based in the south-east of England – in good times and bad – favour London more than they do Wales. The Government has spent astronomical amounts of money bailing out the banking sector based in London – and done nothing for the steel industry, for the car industry or for construction. What we have seen in the last year is the biggest regional redistribution in recent political history: from the poor to the rich, from west to east and south.

Even in future decisions, the needs of Wales are never very high on the London Government's list of priorities. The Severn Barrage could produce 5% of the UK's electricity needs but there are major concerns as to the environmental impact this will have on the habitats along our southern coast. Yet the report by the Government's adviser on the project, PWC, doesn't even mention Wales. And even if it is funded entirely by private finance, the report assumes that ownership of the barrage will revert to the UK Government, which stands to benefit from tens of billions in revenue over the lifetime of the project. All we in Wales will get will be a few construction jobs at the beginning and a few maintenance jobs thereafter. As with coal in the nineteenth and twentieth centuries, so it's destined to be with Wales' rich renewable resource in the twenty-first – our environment will bear the cost, but the profits will be made by others. If we allow this to happen, it will become our Tryweryn.

We must not and will not allow it to happen. They may see us as such, but we are no longer a colonised people – because the days in which our voices can be ignored are gone. The world has moved on and Wales has moved with it. And we are still moving. And so are all the other small nations that are today on the march.

In the island nation of Sardinia our sister party, the Sardinian Action Party, is now a member of the Governing

Coalition. We salute their success. The incoming President of the Government, Ugo Cappellacci, has demanded a new Statute of Autonomy because he says Sardinia is a nation with its own territory, history, language, traditions, culture, identity and aspirations. Cappellacci's party is of the centre-right but he's clearly read his Gramsci.

Italy itself is to become a fully fledged federal state, and soon the province of South-Tyrol – self-governing since 1948 – will have powers of which we in Wales at the moment can only dream: 90% fiscal autonomy and primary law-making powers in many areas. The Tyroleans are asking now for control over the post office. If we had had that power then we wouldn't have had forced closures of local post offices and the forced privatisation of Royal Mail.

Brittany, the land of our cousins, which lost its independence just four years before us in 1532 – may finally be reunited after its division at the hands of the Vichy Government. The historic capital of Nantes, twinned with this, our much younger capital of Cardiff, may finally be coming home if Édouard Balladur's Committee, looking at redrawing the map of France's territorial divisions, sticks to its proposals. Ten thousand have marched in Nantes to end the scandal of partition. Of course, France will not give up without a struggle. This month six young Bretons who sprayed graffiti for Breton unity on public buildings and a TGV have been fined €30,000 and given a suspended two-month jail sentence as punishment. I don't need to remind you of the honourable role played by the paint pot in the history of our movement. For the Bretons, too, '*daw dydd y bydd mawr y rhai bychain*' ('The day will come when the weak will be mighty'), as Waldo Williams once wrote.

Cornwall too is poised to be reunited this year, with the creation of a single Cornish tier of government. The long and convincing campaign by the Cornish Constitutional Convention fought hard to deliver a full-blown Assembly. Yet the London government, with the full backing of the Lib Dems, have imposed a watered-down unitary authority. Nevertheless, at least Cornwall will be one again – and we wish our sister party, Mebyon Kernow, well in this year's elections.

'Remember Cornwall' has long been a chilling slogan in the Celtic lands because of the way in which that country was dismembered. And despite all our recent achievements as a nation and as a movement over recent years, these words of the Cornish political activist Len Truran, spoken thirty years ago, resonate for us in Wales even now:

> What fools we Cornish are: kick us, humiliate us, usurp our power, steal our jobs, rape our countryside and buy up our homes and what do we do? We turn out and vote for the centralist parties that have never done us any good, are doing us no good, will never do us any good.

Well, Wales: this summer is your chance to chart a different course for yourselves.

The nineteenth century experienced a great Springtime of Nations as the revolutions of 1848 saw new countries created the length and breadth of Europe. In our world today we are seeing our own Spring Awakening. People and cultures that have long been dormant and subdued are asserting their right to exist, their right to dream. Take the great post-imperial state of Spain. Underway is a struggle between the old nationalism of the central imperial state and the new nationalism of the stateless nations that are founding their own state. Those who have been without a voice are finding new expression.

In the historic nation of Catalonia a mass movement has taken to the streets to demand the right to self-determination and specifically to call for the right to hold a referendum on the constitutional position of Catalonia. Four thousand Catalans even marched in Brussels to demand a referendum, such is the strength of their desire for democracy, freedom and respect.

The Basques too have been denied their rights: the Ibarretxe Plan for Basque self-autonomy has been declared unconstitutional by the Spanish Courts – the same courts that banned three Basque nationalist parties (all of whom have renounced violence) from taking part in the recent elections, effectively handing electoral victory to the Spanish nationalist parties. Well, we say this to the Spanish Socialist Workers' Party that is now to form a Government with the Conservative Partido Popular: Franco never succeeded in breaking the spirit of the Basques and neither shall you.

In Galicia, where our sister party lost just one seat but is now replaced by the PP in government, the first act of the Spanish nationalists was to end support for the Galician-language nursery schools (the *Galescolas*) unless they are, in their words, 'depoliticised'. So if you teach in Spanish, it's education, but if you teach in Galician, it's ideology. A statement that is worthy of the unreconstructed wing of the British Labour Party. Will the Galicians simply slip back into the shadows of history? Well, that is not what twenty-first century Celts do. Forget the dying Gaul – the bittersweet poetry of disappointment and defeat. The lines we are writing now are ones of praise, of passion, of victory and celebration.

Of course, no nation or party can be without its setbacks, disappointments – disagreements even. But let's never confuse disagreement on policy with a conflict between personalities. This Party needs its Éamon de Valera and it needs its Michael Collins. But let us not make their tragic error and create enmity between all of us who are joined in the common cause of freedom for our country. And to those who feel disheartened when our Government gets it wrong, don't get angry – get even more involved in the democracy of this Party. Submit your motions. Stand for election. Write the manifesto. And if you get elected, reread it.

Welsh nationalists do not have the luxury of resignation. We are a small country that needs the skills of everyone committed to the cause of Wales. We cannot resile from our responsibility as patriots and citizens. And this is not a time to be disheartened. For the truth is, we are the only generation ever in Welsh history that has its destiny within its own hands. Let's seize that opportunity with those hands. Not to demand a referendum will be a vote of no confidence, not in our Government but in our own nation.

Our friends in other small nations are fighting, hoping and marching in capitals across the Continent. Are we not inspired by their example? When we marched here in our capital on St David's Day, were we not a nation transformed from the one that trudged thirty years ago to the day to vote itself out of existence? Do not let the fear of our yesterday snuff out the hope of our tomorrow. If the people of Greenland can turn out and vote by 76% in favour of greater autonomy in the middle of November in the Arctic Circle in freezing temperatures, surely we in Wales can find a little of their determination so that we, like them, can begin to control our own land, our own coast.

Pass over Greenland to the Americas and witness a continent where the indigenous peoples are coming in from the cold. In Bolivia, Evo Morales became the first indigenous government leader in five centuries since the Conquistadors spread death, disease and religion at the point of a gun. In a referendum in January a new constitution was approved which enshrines the right of indigenous people to self-government, and gives their languages, 36 in all, official status. Peoples like the Chima, Yuracaré and Mojeño are exercising their autonomy and their languages have been recognised. We in Wales salute them.

As some peoples emerge blinking into this new dawn of equality, democracy and respect for diversity, the picture for others is not so good. Many thousands of the Saharawi people remain refugees in encampments in Algeria, but they still dream defiantly of a return to their own free and independent land. And we salute them too.

The Tamils of Tamil Eelam are undergoing daily waves of attacks and repression at the hands of the Sri Lankan Government which bear all the hallmarks of genocide. The world is silent. But we will not forget you. In West Papua – illegally annexed by Indonesia in 1963 – thousands are demonstrating on the streets for independence, in a country where even to fly the West Papuan flag is to risk a prison sentence.

These examples of courage and commitment in the face of terrible risks inspire us. But Eluned Morgan – retiring from the European Parliament to spend more time with her karaoke machine – says nationalism is an evil and that those who desire freedom for their countries are to be despised, not admired. Well, I say tell that to the Tamils, the West Papuans, and tell it to the spirits of Kossuth, Masaryk, Kenyatta, Gandhi, Simón Bolívar, José Martí… and all the liberators in human history.

Of course, there are those Labour politicians – another MEP whose name I have forgotten springs to mind – who will support independence movements anywhere else in the world apart from their known country. Now, Peter Hain has added a new twist to Labour and declared they do support Welsh independence after all, but only in the fifteenth century. Oh, and he does support a referendum on law-making powers, just not in the twenty-first century.

This is the crux of it: what kind of Wales do we want to be? A nation like the Basque Country or Catalonia, on the march to equality among the nations of the world? Or a cowed, unconfident country, unsure of its past, uncertain of its future?

There was a man once who saw Wales' future as an independent country in a Europe of nations. At the 1988 Machynlleth Festival, which launched the most colourful European election campaign that we have ever run – with Jill Evans among the candidates – Gwyn Alf Williams enjoined us to follow Glyndŵr to the end of the rainbow. 'Join Glyndŵr's Army' is not quite as colourful as a phrase, but if Labour wants to turn people into nationalists, then fair enough – they've been doing it without trying for 70 years.

That European election turned round the fortunes of this Party. It ended a decade of decline that began in 1979. It taught us to believe again. The Europe of 1989, with the fall of Communism, was a brighter, more optimistic world than the Europe of today, beset by economic woes. But in among the gloom shine tiny points of light.

There has of course been much glee in Labour circles of late at the travails of Iceland and Ireland, as if the UK is somehow a paragon of economic virtue. All the more remarkable then that Greenland, that other north Atlantic island, can vote yes to greater self-government at this time. If they can still show resources of hope and a solid rock of self-belief with just 50,000 souls, then how much more should we, with sixty times that number. If they can refresh and renew, if they can be a green land, then so can Wales too.

Four years ago this Party began to turn itself around. We chose the poppy as a symbol of the unity of our country – a hardy flower as happy growing on the slopes of Snowdon as it is in suburban gardens or the cracks in the pavement of a Valleys street. It is the only poppy indigenous to Europe, a symbol of Wales' heritage as one of the oldest of all European nations. The Celts were once the fathers of Europe; but now all we want is to be members in our own right of the great European family. So let us fight this election beneath this flag and reach out our arms to brother and sister nations, small and large, old and new, as equals – not just on this island but in this continent and throughout the world. We have nothing to lose but our lack of belief. We have a Wales to win.

17

That temporary Parliament on the banks of the Thames

Plaid Cymru Autumn Conference, Llandudno – 2009

CONFERENCE, I SHALL never forget that clear June morning in 2001 when a band of my most loyal lieutenants were waiting to travel up with me to London for the first time, like Gwynfor all those years ago – though we were going by bus, not by train, and they didn't name it after me. Some of them are in the hall today. They were early, or I was late – probably the latter as there were more of them than me. No matter, this was one trip that literally couldn't leave without me.

We met at dawn in the village of Ferryside – a fitting choice, looking back, as it was the home of Hugh Williams, the radical lawyer and Chartist, some even say the instigator of what came to be known as the Rebecca Riots, but was actually an uprising. In 1839, the year of that other rising in Newport, he published a volume of National Songs which included these stirring words by the Tycroes poet Thomas Jenkins:

Sons of Cambria – come arise,
And no longer be
Serfs enslaved...
Burst your shackles – and be free
Sons of Cambria – follow me!

The 'me' in the text is Liberty – the one thing this nation has lacked longest and needed most, the noblest of all human aspirations: the desire to be free. Free to be ourselves, to speak our language, to celebrate our culture, free from poverty and disease, free to live in peace, to shape our own future, to make our own mistakes and claim our own successes. Free from the shadow of Westminster awaiting us that fine June day.

In the first few days I was in the House of Commons, before I even gave my maiden speech, I remember Tommy McAvoy, a gruff but affable Glaswegian who is still the Deputy Chief Whip, beckoning me over in the Members' Lobby and taking me up to the roof of the Palace. And as he pointed reverently to St Paul's and Lambeth Palace and the Treasury Building, with Big Ben towering over us, he said, "This, Adam, is why I am ay Unionist, proud to call myself British". I am sure this was intended as an act of kindness, but for a moment I had flashbacks – half-digested Sunday School stories of the Devil tempting Christ at the pinnacle of the Temple, mixed in with the murder scene with Francis Urquhart from the TV series *House of Cards*.

I made my excuses and left. That the Labour Party should try and recruit me is a compliment of sorts, I suppose. They thought I was a prodigal son – now I think they would be less charitable, and question my legitimacy. Baroness Gale of Blaenrhondda – a name to conjure with if ever there was one – has often over the years asked me, in a voice seductive as the sexy temptress Gossamer Beynon in *Under Milk Wood*, when I was "coming home to Labour". In my case, I think we can say she was miscast, misinformed and Miss-downright-impertinent.

Well, I tell you: I do want to come home. To my real home, my Welsh home. It's not just that I'm tired of the travelling – as someone once said, that's the problem with London: it's so damned far away from everywhere. I am tired of hitting my head and my hand against the dumb cold walls of Westminster. I will never feel that I belong in that Parliament, though I have to breathe its dust-laden air. I want a Parliament which belongs to me and to us. A Parliament that we have built in whose stones our horizons sing – *creu gwir fel gwydr o ffwrnais awen.*

The Palace of Westminster is undeniably an imposing and impressive building. It is an architectural metaphor for the British political system. Its symbol, after all, is a portcullis – it is a fortress designed to keep the people out and the power in. And just as the cathedral builders of the middle ages sought to make us feel small in the presence of almighty God, Westminster's subliminal message is that we as citizens are of no significance when compared with the power and majesty of the state. As Aneurin Bevan said in *In Place of Fear:*

> The House of Commons is like a church. The vaulted roofs and
> stained glass windows, the rows of statues of great statesmen
> of the past, the echoing halls, the soft-footed attendants and the
> whispered conversations... he [the newly elected MP] is expected
> to worship; and in the most conservative of all religions – ancestor
> worship.

Except they are not even our ancestors.

Who can blame the Welsh MP from a working-class constituency who feels a little bit out of their depth? Cloisters in Wales are a rare Sunday-afternoon treat on a coach trip to St Davids. To members of the British Establishment, they are the familiar architecture that has punctuated their very life history: from prep school to Eton, to Oxbridge, the Guards or the Inns of Court, then the Commons, and finally the Lords.

Before you know it, you've changed your accent, your dress and your values to fit in. J H Thomas, the rail union leader from Newport, tried so hard he took to wearing evening dress even at eleven o'clock in the morning. They made him Colonial Secretary – not once but twice. Nobody does imperialism quite like a self-denying member of a conquered nation.

Even now there are Labour MPs who wander the corridors of power with that peculiar fixed smile on their face of the permanently self-satisfied, unable to believe their luck in just Being There, kitted out in matching silk ties, silk hankies and for all I know, silk underwear as well – they are so effortlessly smooth. You wouldn't guess the conflict that lies just beneath the surface from constantly flipping their loyalty back and forth from Wales to London, like flipping a coin or flipping a home on expenses. Home is, after all, where the heart is.

Like many of the people in it, the building itself is a grand deception: designed to look centuries older than it is in order to confer upon it the gravitas of history. Everything about that building, everything it represents – and for sure the one thing it does *not* represent is the ordinary Welsh voter – is a fraud from crenellated top to bottom. It is corrupt and corrupting – no building where an army of flunkies opens doors for the privileged few can be healthy – and the sooner we get out of it, the better it will be for all of us.

But while we are there we have to have someone fight our corner. In Elfyn Llwyd we have a magnificent general, as strong as an oak and as wise as an owl. But while he has two able lieutenants, if I may say so myself, what he really needs is an army to defend Wales from injustice, to field our best questions, to marshal our best arguments, not to drive home our own advantage but to secure victory on the political battlefield for Wales. Because battlefield the Welsh political landscape will inevitably become over the next few years, and we will need every ounce of self-belief to sustain us.

After a decade of lost opportunity and hopeless ineffectiveness, we are now on the cusp of a new decade: of conflict, of cuts and conservatism. In one sense a change of the guard at Westminster makes little difference to us. Wales has suffered under Labour and we've suffered under the Conservatives. The only way to stop suffering is to get out from under them, and believe me, we will in 2011.

But I suppose there is some subtle difference: while Labour governments never fail to disappoint you, Conservative governments confirm your worst nightmare. This will be the 67th Conservative government in history, which, considering they have never in living memory had a majority of Welsh MPs, is a little bit troubling from the perspective of Welsh democracy.

Tory governments have never come highly recommended in Wales. If you go back far enough, they were a coalition of Publicans and Anglicans and anglicised absentee landlords – the original unholy alliance. The Conservative and Unionist Party in Wales has never really recovered from these rather inauspicious beginnings. They have been on the wrong side of every important argument for the last three hundred years: the Reform Act, the welfare state, the NHS, apartheid, the NHS again. Name virtually any issue, any cause that has taxed the minds (and frequently the bodies too) of the people of this country for the last three centuries, and the Tories have always somehow managed to place themselves squarely on the side of privilege and prejudice – on the opposite side to the majority of the downtrodden Welsh, so much so that the very term Welsh Conservative still creaks under the heavy weight of a deep historical contradiction.

When Rebecca rode out in Carmarthenshire to burn the hated toll booths, where were the Tories? Not on the side of the farmers struggling to survive, but the men of property, the turnpike owners – the PFI merchants of their day – turning a quick profit at the people's expense. Political cross-dressers, Peter Mandelson please note, are progressives in our tradition. I once called Dafydd Elis-Thomas the pantomime dame of Welsh politics and he thanked me for the compliment.

The Tories are democracy's late developers. Opposed to extending the franchise at every juncture, if it had been down to them, women and the working classes would never have had the vote – which goes a long way to explaining Leanne Wood's attitude. Thank God for women with attitude. The Tories opposed the secret ballot and saw to it that those who didn't vote the right way were evicted. They opposed the repeal of the Corn Laws when people were starving not just in Ireland but also in Wales. They opposed the Methodist Revival, supported religious discrimination against Nonconformists but demanded they paid church taxes and attended Anglican schools – though not Anglican universities, from which they were banned. They opposed the Disestablishment of the Church of Wales, despite it being the will of the majority in our country at the time.

But then opposing Welsh democracy is written into the DNA of Conservative tradition: they have opposed every Welsh devolution bill in history – a record not even the Labour Party can compete with. They opposed redoubtable E T John's Government of Wales Bill on the brink of the First World War. They opposed mighty S O Davies' bill in the 1950s. They opposed the Wales Act in 1978 and took great delight in removing it from the Statute Book with an Order in Council as soon as they were elected. They made opposition to devolution the cornerstone of their 1997 campaign and were wiped out in Wales as a consequence, yet still sought to frustrate the wishes of the Welsh people by voting against the bill in Parliament. And who can forget Nick Bourne beaming before Carmarthenshire's votes were counted, thinking that Wales had yet again collectively voted itself out of existence for the second time in our history, choosing the life of a vassal, not a victor. I never want to see a smile like that again. No man who betrayed his country so enthusiastically could ever earn the right to lead it.

True to form, the Welsh Conservative Party opposed the Government of Wales Act 2006 – like every one before it – and no doubt they will campaign NO come next year's referendum.

They are the party of the Union – a Union imposed on Wales without a vote. For the Union, and against the development of our Welsh democracy, every step of our own Welsh way.

The Tories now claim to be Wales' new best friend – but this is difficult to take when for so long they have been our worst enemy. They fought the Welsh miners – seeking to grind them like the coal on the slag-heaps into dust – in 1926, in 1973 and 1984. They privatised our steelworks not once but twice, and threw thousands on the dole. And then there was Tryweryn, a scar on the conscience of the Tories as deep and as powerful in its own way as Aberfan was for Labour: both of them symbols of human suffering at the hands of a distant and uncaring government. *Cofiwch Dryweryn*, and above all remember that when the Liverpool Corporation Bill had its second reading, the Conservative Minister for Welsh Affairs stubbornly sided with Liverpool over Wales despite the fact that every Welsh MP opposed it. The Conservative Government placed a three-line whip on the destruction of a community. When the political epitaph of the Conservative Party in Wales comes to be written, let it never be forgotten that they were responsible for the greatest act of neo-colonial vandalism in our history.

And if they want our forgiveness, then let David Cameron apologise to the Welsh people for their mistake. He apologised about apartheid. He apologised to the gay community over Section 28 – or at least to a £50-a-ticket invitation-only Conservative-supporting section of the gay community in London's most expensive members' club – I'd like to see him trying say sorry to a roomful of Valleys drag queens (you know who you are). Well, if Cameron is in the habit of apologising, he can try apologising to the people of Capel Celyn, Meirionnydd and Wales for a village drowned and a democracy disregarded. And then promise to give us – like the Scots, the English and the Irish – and any other nation, control over our own water in our own land. Or are we still to be treated as England's first and final precious piece of Empire?

Of course, it's possible to be Welsh and small 'c' conservative. What is cultural nationalism but an attempt to conserve and preserve for future generations the best in our own traditions? The problem with Conservatism as a political philosophy is that it is defined by what it is against: change. And when you live in a country like ours, calling out for change: who would want to slow change down, to be a brake on progress?

In 300 years the Tories in Wales have only been anti-Establishment once, when Sir Watkin Williams-Wynn harboured a certain affection for Bonnie Prince Charlie, but not so much as to risk a martyr's death at Culloden. I am more Jacobin than Jacobite – but there's room enough in our Party for the creative intelligence of a David Melding, one of nature's conservatives, maybe – a man who once told me he hadn't yet got over the shock of the Reformation. Join us, David, the water's warm... You are living proof that it is possible to be a Welsh Conservative but, boy, it must be mentally exhausting. Trying to be both in capital letters of equal measure must be as impossible as serving two masters.

And for the Tories' masters in London, time and time again we've learned: Wales will never be the priority. They have already said they will cancel the electrification of the Great Western Main Line to west Wales, happy to acquiesce in the pathetic fact that Wales is almost alone in the western world in lacking a single line of electrified rail track – though the City of London will get its coveted Crossrail. The Tories announced with a fanfare that they will build a new high-speed rail line connecting London and the Continent with Manchester, Birmingham and Leeds – but Cardiff and Swansea must wait. Wales – under the Tories – will always have to wait.

And there will be no high-speed return for the brave Welsh warriors of Helmand when they are sent back out again. The party that has supported every war in British history – from the concentration camps of Pretoria to the lies of Suez and Iraq – will continue with the war in Afghanistan.

And instead of a war on poverty, the Tories will declare war on the poor. They will cut the money Wales gets from the Lottery – scrapping the only Lottery fund that gives Wales money according to a needs-based formula. They will cut public spending, hitting Wales hard – and continue to justify the unjust Barnett Formula. And they proudly promise they will slash the benefits of hundreds of thousands of Welsh claimants in the middle of the biggest economic crash since the Thirties. Let's repeat that. The party that gave us the Means Test plan to cull one and a half million people from incapacity benefit in just twelve months, more than ten times the rate even New Labour has achieved. The long-term unemployed, single parents and the clinically depressed will be dragooned into community service like criminals, or lose benefits and starve. This is the modern equivalent of the workhouse and the abolition of outdoor relief. It will hit Wales hard. And it will hurt the young and the very old hardest of all.

The man the Tories have charged with implementing this policy of socio-economic 'shock and awe', Lord Freud – up until February an adviser on welfare reform to New Labour, so obviously a man of principle – has the qualification of having been one of those very investment bankers that trashed our economy and slung so many people on the scrapheap. By his own admission, thousands of investors lost money in Eurotunnel because, naively, they believed what this silver-tongued ex-journalist – dubbed Fraud Squad by his colleagues – told them. Who said an end to the politics of spin?

So maybe it's time to dust down one of Bevan's other great works, written under the suitably patriotic pseudonym Celticus: *Why Not Trust The Tories?* If any one doubts the contemporary relevance of a pamphlet written in 1944, then read the section where Bevan talks about the Tories' tendency to "smooth away the edge of policy in the hope of making it more attractive to doubtful supporters". It's almost as if he has read every Conservative policy commission in the last two years. David Cameron, by his own admission, is the "heir to Blair" – he represents not change but more of the same, and worse. Except where Blair appointed a former *Mirror* Editor as his foul-mouthed mouthpiece, Cameron has appointed a disgraced former Editor of the *News of the World*.

This Labour Government is a failed and dying government. Its sins are too many for it to die an honourable death. So let it die. The same is true of a so-called Mother of Parliaments that failed to stop those sins. The only thing that can wash them away is new blood – not the real blood of those brave souls in Afghanistan and Iraq that have paid dearly for politicians' errors, but the new blood of a new politics. There will be new MPs aplenty in this Parliament, so many that the maiden speeches will last for months. Will the politics change along with the personnel? For England's sake I hope it is a new start, a Maiden Parliament, though somehow I doubt it, as power's old habits die hard – but for us in Wales it must neither be Maiden nor Mother, but Midwife to a Parliament of our own.

There have been about a thousand Welsh MPs from the Act of Union onwards, and, from a strictly Welsh perspective, most of them have been practically useless. In that sense, the present crop are no better nor worse than previous generations – though I cannot quite imagine Emlyn Hooson moonlighting for the *Daily Sport*.

The difference lies within Wales itself, a nation in which the old order is dying and the new is struggling to be born. For that new birth we need a new breed of Members for Wales in that temporary Parliament along the banks of the Thames, who will never go native in exile and never play by other people's rules... members like the One True Original Member for Carmarthen who broke the conventions of the House – who in his first act of defiance sat down on the Treasury Bench until the original language of these islands was given due recognition in the only Parliament we had, who committed the cardinal sin of injecting passion and politics into his first address to the

House. And maybe one or two like this one, who got slung out of Parliament for calling a liar a liar.

As Plaid MPs, we don't go to London to scale the escalator of ambition. For every Welsh MP, Parliament in a faraway capital should seem like a prison, though they try and paint our chains in gold. Penri, Dylan, Myfanwy, here is the only reason you want to be there, the reason we hold dear – to bring democracy home to where it belongs: in the hands of our people, in our Parliament, in our capital, in our country. In our dreams for the moment. But in our destiny too.

18

A fo ben, bid bont – Let he (or she) that would be leader, be a bridge

Translation of column in *Golwg* magazine
– 12 March, 2009

"IN THE YEAR of our Lord 1531," say the Chronicles of Hywel ap Syr Mathew, "Rh. Ap Gr. lost his head." This is an abbreviation of Rhys ap Gruffydd ap Urien, one of the Lords of Dinefwr, who I referred to this week on Plaid's new website on independence – www.walescan.org. What is the significance of this man, who was executed on the morning of 4th December 1531, aged just 23? Well, firstly the fact that so few know about him speaks volumes about the way we are deprived of our history as a nation. But mainly because his crime was trying to make himself, according to the verdict in his trial, the prince of an independent Wales.

This Rhys was the grandson of Sir Rhys ap Thomas, the Tudors' chief supporter in Wales and the man who did more than almost anyone else to put the 'Son of Prophecy', Henry Tudor, on the British throne. The dream turned sour for

Wales and the Dinefwr family within a generation. Henry VII appointed an Englishman, Lord Ferrers, ahead of Rhys to the governorship of south Wales and displayed the first signs of the centralising tendencies of the Anglo-British state that, to some extent, remain with us today. Rhys refused to accept Henry VIII's anti-Welshness, or his anti-Catholicism. Rhys was therefore not just a nationalist martyr but the first Catholic martyr in England's Protestant Reformation. His uncle, James ap Gruffydd ap Hywel, was the first Catholic spy from England to go to the continent: in search, perhaps, of Papal support for an uprising in Wales.

As a family whose own rise to power was steeped in legend, myth was a central feature of the Tudor court. The indictment against Rhys spoke of an old prophecy that ravens and the red hand would defeat the King of England. The Dinefwr coat of arms was three ravens – the red hand perhaps referred to Owain Lawgoch ('Owain Redhand'), or to Ulster, which was in revolt at the time. Rhys lost his head on Tower Hill or the White Hill where, according to the *Mabinogi*, the head of Brân ('Raven'), the King of legends, was buried. Rhys was also a descendant of Urien Rheged: it was Urien's head that Llywarch Hen tried to prevent from falling into his enemies' hands.

This young man's head was lost (like many of his compatriots before him – Llywelyn *Ein Llyw Olaf* ('Our Last Leader'), Rhys Ddu ('Black Rhys') and Rhys ap Tudur – because he challenged England's political authority. Within a few years, the remainder of Welsh independence was lost too – Hywel Dda's laws (written in Dinefwr), the language and what was our religion at that time. Rhys' execution was the first act of Union.

To some extent the history of the two Rhyses – one showing fealty to London and the other his loyalty to Wales – depicts the choice that every generation has faced in the years since. The only difference now is that no-one is going to put our head on a spike. We are the masters of our own future, if we choose to be. *A fo ben, bid bont* – let he (or she) that would be leader, be a bridge.

19

Ammanford's egghead

Translation of column in *Golwg* magazine – 18 May, 2009

"AMMANFORD'S LEADING EGGHEAD – and Eisteddfod shock-jock" was the First Minister's playful description of me in his final speech as leader of the Labour Party. It's a badge I would wear with pride, although I'm not sure I deserve it. There's a slight hint of metropolitan snobbery in the charge, of course; the suggestion that the whole concept of intelligentsia in the Amman Valley is a bit of fun. It reminds me of the old squabble between Saunders Lewis and W J Gruffydd, I believe between the two wars, about to what extent it was possible to be a modern intellectual as much in, say, Carmarthen as in Paris. To both of them, I'm sure that Aberystwyth would have been fine. *Plus ça change.*

Around the turn of the twentieth century, Ammanford was the home of the White House, an important meeting place for anarchists and socialists under the patronage of George Davidson, the millionaire Managing Director of Kodak UK. It was the beginning of the impressive record of this small area, attracted to trade unionism comparatively late, for producing radical leaders in the twentieth century. The two most famous were Jim Griffiths from Betws, Wales' first Secretary of State and creator of the first national insurance scheme, and D J Davies from Carmel, one of the most important thinkers in Plaid Cymru's early history.

I can't describe Neil Hamilton, the former Conservative minister who went to Amman Valley Grammar School, as any sort of egghead. However, one who went to the same primary school as me in Tycroes is sure to count: Alan Watkins, one of the best political commentators there ever was. Unfortunately, his few comments about Ammanford were damning and humbling: he described depression as being 'a wet afternoon in a place called Ammanford', and he spoke about the tendency of Ammanford folk to drag their feet with everything, about doing things 'tomorrow' – and 'tomorrow' meaning the same as in Spanish, "but without the suggestion of haste".

The truth is that anyone can feign sophistication in London or Cardiff. The real achievement is being an intellectual who represents something: with roots, with a sense of perspective. I remember Philip Weekes, former head of British Coal, saying that in west Wales he came across the most polished union leaders, with the chapel and *Das Kapital* entwined in a victorious synthesis. If I am half as good as that, my small contribution to the national discourse won't be entirely in vain.

20

Why we need devolution in reverse

The Welsh Agenda – Winter 2012

IT'S 80 YEARS since events in Spain galvanised an entire political generation in Wales. The winds of change we are witnessing today in Bilbao and Barcelona may prove every bit as defining for the emerging twenty-first-century generation of Welsh leaders. As I write, a majority in favour of independence has already been elected in the Basque Country and in Catalonia. Even Galicia, which remained loyal to the centralist Partido Popular of its native son and Spanish Premier Mariano Rajoy, saw nationalist parties achieving almost a quarter of the votes, a near-historic high. In Flanders the pro-independence N-VA has just taken control of Antwerp City Council, a potent symbol of their likely victory in the 2014 Federal Elections. Meanwhile, members of the Regional Council of Veneto have voted 42-18 to hold an EU-monitored referendum within the year to become a sovereign republic within the EU. Given this constellation of events, it's difficult to avoid the conclusion that the tectonic plates of Europe's political map are shifting. For so long a Utopian dream, the breakdown of nations once prophesied by the Austrian visionary Leopold Kohr and the Breton advocate of *L'Europe aux Cent Drapeaux*, Yann Fouéré, at long last seems close to becoming a reality. And then, of course, there is Scotland. How fitting it is that a descendant of the Cameron clan, fervent Jacobites all, should help pave the way back to Scottish independence. Even more ironic is the fact that David Cameron's success over the next two years will be the biggest factor in determining the outcome of the referendum vote.

Polled recently by *The Sunday Times*, a majority of Scots said they would vote for independence if they thought the Conservative-Lib Dem Coalition would be returned at the next Westminster election. That result depends upon the prospects of an economic recovery. George Osborne's green shoots may yet supply the SNP their victory laurels.

But what does this mean for us in Wales? Well, don't discount the possibility of some kind of domino effect. It's happened before. A little over a year after Scottish independence was secured at Bannockburn, the Welsh in Glamorgan rose in rebellion under Llywelyn Bren. Edward Bruce, the King of Scotland's brother, wrote to the Welsh offering to help liberate them from the Norman yoke. Sir Gruffydd Llwyd wrote back to say that the Welsh were happy to accept. Llwyd was arrested for attempting to make Edward Bruce, already Overlord of Ireland, Prince of Wales in a Celtic Empire to rival the emerging Anglo-Norman state.

Modern Wales is far removed from the tribulations of the fourteenth century. But the parallels are intriguing. In its current form, the United Kingdom is a carefully constructed constitutional balancing act, which nevertheless only functions through the tacit acceptance by the minority nations of the Celtic Rim that the Centre of Power ultimately reigns supreme. Challenge that – as Bruce and Wallace did in 1314 – and the whole unwieldy structure can soon come tumbling down.

But herein lies the problem. The Mexican wave of

independentisme sweeping through western Europe from the Ramblas to Renfrewshire is limited to those stateless nations that are more advanced economically than the central state they are seeking to leave. This is a club of the successful-yet-stateless, membership of which we in Wales can only aspire.

When a youthful Dafydd Wigley, Phil Williams and Eurfyl ap Gwilym sat down to write their classic Economic Plan for Wales in 1970, we could boast a level of income of about 92% of the UK average. Factoring in lower inflation, higher amenity value (Wales is, after all, a beautiful country) and with some well-targeted pruning of an overweening defence and foreign affairs budget, then self-government (as it was called then) was an imaginative but realistic political project. Today we are caught in the constitutional equivalent of Catch 22. Lack of self-government – and the levers of economic power it supplies – has immiserated the Welsh economy to just 73% of the UK GVA per head. We need the powers of independence to prise us from this rut, but are deemed too poor to afford them.

This need not be a manifesto for Welsh miserabilism. So what is the alternative? Wales needs a grand historical compromise between what I call 'practical nationalism' and 'progressive Unionism'. On the economic front, this means a pact to drive Welsh prosperity back up to levels close to the average in these islands. For nationalists, this will be a platform of self-confidence for future independence. For unionists, this may represent a closer economic integration with the rest of Britain. May the best narrative win. What matters is our ability to deliver, say, half a dozen transformational policies and mega-projects that can drive up our growth rate by 1% a year over the next 20 years. We need to do this whatever happens in the rest of the island. The Scottish people may end up sending something of a mixed message to the political class – as the Québécois did in 1980, and even more so in 1995 – in the words of the great René Lévesque, the urbane, chain-smoking Premier of Québec, voting "yes, but not yet". But if the break-up of Britain comes before the end of the decade, then we in Wales will need to display a degree of intellectual agility. A union of England-and-Wales simply will not work – look up binationalism and Austria-Hungary to work out why. Yet, for the majority at least, independence is a step too far at this stage in our political evolution. Which is why we need a meaningful interim arrangement.

Getting agreement on that will require what Lévesque called a *"beau risque"* between nationalists and unionists, to create in Gwyn Alf Williams' term a "Commonwealth of Wales". This will be constitutionally sovereign but, in international law, in free association with the successor British state. We would choose to share with Britain-wide institutions, including a directly elected confederal Parliament, those areas where the continuation of common policies would be in our own interest.

In other words, devolution in reverse. The Commonwealth of Wales – like those other halfway houses, the Irish Free State and the Dominions of Australia and Canada – will give us self-determination without separation, and the power to build up our wealth in common. It's an opportunity we can ill afford to squander.

21

The glacial speed of
Welsh progress

Translation of column in *Golwg* magazine
– 19 August, 2009

REREADING K O Morgan's *Rebirth of a Nation* the other day, I came across a reference to Labour's five priorities for Wales in their 1945 General Election literature. They were:

- "a Secretary of State" – not created till 1964, soon to be abolished by the Tories.

- "a separate Welsh Broadcasting Corporation" – not really ever fully realised, even now. A Welsh Broadcasting Council was created in 1953 to oversee the output of the BBC; Teledu Cymru flickered into life for two years in the early 60s, and, in the Welsh language, of course, S4C was established – reluctantly – in 1983. But the fact that we are still waiting for overall control of media in Wales, more than 50 years on, is to be seen in the current campaign for a Media Commission for Wales – supported by the Welsh Government, but opposed/ignored by Whitehall.

- "an end to the forced transfer of labour from Wales to England" – this was something more commonly associated with the Nazis and their *Zwangsarbeiter* in Poland. Presumably the reference is to redundant miners and steelworkers being offered transfers to England – a practice which did continue, I think, beyond World War II. Nowadays the Labour Government is busy with the 'forced transfer' of ex-miners and steelworkers from Incapacity Benefit to the cheaper ESA.

- "a central body to plan and develop the Welsh economy" – this took 30 years to achieve, with the creation of the Welsh Development Agency. The WDA rose to become one of the most respected economic development bodies in the world. Then the Labour Party abolished it. Some people think we should bring it back – I tend to agree.

- "a new north-south Wales trunk road". Half a century later and for large parts of the route, the A470 remains more of a figment of the national imagination than a road in the conventional sense. At least the present Transport Minister is finally getting to grips with Labour's unfinished business.

What is really striking about the last point is that Labour were passionate about north-south links in 1945 where now, if they mention them at all, it is to attack them as a dangerous nationalist obsession.

The reason for the change of heart as far as Labour is concerned is obvious: then they were just as much a north Wales party as a south Wales party, thanks to the coal miners of the north-east and the quarrymen of the north-west. They were, in other words, a genuinely pan-Wales party, whereas now, as Richard Wyn Jones persuasively argues in the magazine *Barn* ('Opinion'), they are fast becoming a regional party within Wales, confined to the post-industrial south. An interesting titbit within the article: which are the only two parties in Wales that received more than a thousand votes in every constituency during the European elections? The answer: Plaid and UKIP. For all Huw Lewis' protestations about the irrelevance of identity politics, Welsh politics in the twenty-first century will be a battle between Welsh values (including social democratic notions of equality) and reactionary British nationalism. I know which one I want to win; the question to you, Huw, is: do you?

22

It's good to be home

Plaid Cymru Autumn Conference, Aberystwyth – 2015

IT FEELS AS if I have been on something of an extended gap year, which somehow turned into five. Two of those years I spent in an American university. Universities, like monasteries and prisons, are places where you can do a lot of thinking – though, admittedly, there are more distractions.

When I was away, I thought a lot about Wales. Simón Bolívar, who fought and won independence not for one country but three – now, that's ambition for you – once said this: "To understand a revolution, you have to experience it very close and judge it from afar." So I took his advice and moved to Boston, not to understand a revolution but something equally momentous for our small nation: the mysteries of Welsh devolution.

I focused most of my energy on takeaways. I don't mean late-night fast food to get me through an essay crisis. Takeaways in America are key insights that you glean from a book, a lecture or a conversation. And for me the greatest insight of all is this: leadership is about helping people deal with the challenge of change. Without leadership, then we as a society cannot progress.

The poor quality of our politics in Wales eventually feeds through into the quality of our own lives – as fathers and sons, mothers and daughters. We can ignore, but we can't escape the community that binds us. The limits of its ambitions are the horizons of our hope. Just as the possibilities of tomorrow are set by the decisions of today, so a land without leaders soon becomes a desert where the future cannot grow.

In 1999 this felt like a young country. It was a small country that dared to have big dreams. The irrepressible young Rhodri Glyn Thomas prised Carmarthenshire away from a Labour Party that had ruled us without a break for 20 years. But not even we expected Helen in Llanelli, and Geraint in the Rhondda, and Gareth in Aberconwy and Brian in Islwyn. The people of Wales surprised us and probably surprised themselves. That we could do this. That we could decide for ourselves.

In 1999 we outpaced the SNP; within a year we had brought down a First Minister. We should have gone one further and put one forward ourselves – the greatest First Minister that Wales has never had: my friend, Dafydd Wigley.

Next year Wales will have been 20 years in Labour – a new Wales, dying to be born, to thrive, to prosper and to grow. How well is our Wales doing? A reasonable question to ask of any government. Let's judge Labour by those critical measures of wellbeing: how well we learn, live and earn.

Education is an area we might have expected to flourish with devolution. Wales has a long history, after all, as a pioneer. This was no accident. Necessity was for us the grandmother of invention. We were a country beset by poverty, with no government of our own on which to call. We created a better future for our children through collective effort. Think of Griffith Jones, an eighteenth-century vicar in Carmarthenshire, with no resources to draw upon other than his own love of learning, but who created the world's first successful programme of mass adult literacy. His schools taught 150,000 people to read and attracted the interest of international observers from as far afield as the court of Catherine the Great of Russia. In 1889 the Welsh Intermediate Education Act saw the creation of democratically accountable Joint Education Committees – the forerunners of local education authorities – a full 13 years before England. We were the first to build a publicly funded system of school inspection, to see the need for a technical education curriculum to complement the grammar schools and to create a comprehensive school; and here in Aberystwyth we built a university with the pennies of the poor.

That legacy of educational innovation lived on throughout the twentieth century. Despite a crushing burden of desperate poverty, Wales by the dawn of devolution had a record of pupil achievement at 15 years of age equal to anything that England's better-funded schools could boast. Since then our educational-level standing, in these islands and internationally, has gone down and down – so much so that a former Welsh Education Minister, soon-to-be ex-AM for the Rhondda, was forced to admit a 'systemic crisis.' When Welsh Education Ministers talk about closing the attainment gap between England and Wales, remember this – the gap is a gap that they themselves created. The real underachievers in Wales are not students or teachers, they are the Labour Party, which has failed an entire generation of our young people. They've failed the test of leadership and now it's time to give someone else a chance.

The most damning evidence of all is the slide in the international rankings of Welsh 15 year olds' abilities in Reading, Maths and Science. Wales has been tested three times since 2006 and each time we have slid ever further down the league table, well below the international average and well below the other UK nations. Can we as a country, a small country that excels in so many fields – no. 2 in the world in rugby, no. 9 in the world for soccer – content ourselves with 41st in reading and 43rd in maths? The OECD said in its own official report to the Welsh Government last year that the Welsh education system is failing at both ends of the ability spectrum, with "a high proportion of low performers and a low proportion of high performers." In other words, in a few short years Wales has gone from leader to laggard. If the Welsh Government was subject to the kind of assessment that schools and local education authorities are, then there can be no doubt that its Education Ministers would long ago have been placed in special measures.

As the birthplace of the NHS, health is also an area in which we might expect to excel. The picture here, however, is every bit as bad. The 'Gold Standard' in comparing health systems worldwide is 'avoidable deaths'. In Wales the proportion of avoidable deaths in overall deaths remains significantly higher than England. If Wales had kept pace in cutting preventable deaths in recent years with the region in England with the most similar health profile– the north-east – then more than 800 people in Wales every year would avoid unnecessary, premature deaths, with all the heartache that entails. It amounts to thousands of avoidable deaths over the course of the last decade and a half. There are people we knew and loved that would be with us in this room now, and many more at home, if life and death was not the cruel postcode lottery it currently is in Wales for those with chronic conditions. And let there be no doubt that the most chronic condition of all we as a nation face, of course, is the lack of leadership under Labour.

NHS waiting times in Wales are a stain on a nation that has always put the weak and the vulnerable at the front of the queue. By the end of July of this year, 27,313 patients had been waiting more than 36 weeks for their treatment, the highest number on record ever, and an almost fourfold increase since 2011. Labour dismisses this as *Daily Mail* propaganda. You can almost hear the First Minister leaning on his lectern. How out of touch, how arrogant. This isn't Tory propaganda. It's the widely respected Nuffield Foundation, who confirmed in a study last year that waiting times for hip and knee replacements in Wales were on average 100 days longer than in England or

Scotland. It's the Wales Audit Office report, which showed that the average patient in Wales waits about five to six weeks longer than in England, and those waiting the longest wait three and a half months more. Can all these bodies be wrong, and our First Minister be the only one that is right?

Turning to the economy, not much needs to be said. Labour promised us in 1997 that there would be a devolution dividend. We have had the very opposite. Relative to the EU and to the UK, we are worse off now than we were then – down from 85% of the EU per capita GVA in 2000 to 74% in 2011, and from 73.8% of UK average income in 1997 to 72.2% in 2013. The payback for Welsh voters' 20-year-long loyalty to Labour, it seems, has been a negative return on their investment.

It's important to remember that behind these statistics lies the human cost of reduced earnings, lower grades, shortened lives. It's difficult not to be angry. And yes, I want to turn apathy in Wales – the passive resignation that so many of our people feel, that this is as good as it gets – into anger. First into anger and then into hope. Devolution under Labour has failed. And we are the ones to fix it.

The reason for the failure is obvious. By the time of next year's Assembly elections, the Labour Party will have governed Wales at a national level for an unbroken 19 years. This makes it the longest-serving administration of any country in the whole of the European Union. It's not hard to realise why this might be a problem. Every democracy needs the real chance of change. The pendulum swing of an alternative government brings with it new ideas and new leadership, the lifeblood of renewal. The opposite is stasis, inertia, fatigue. *Croeso i Gymru*.

Even the smartest of single-party hegemonies eventually run out of steam. Starved of the oxygen of new ideas, dominant parties become sclerotic, an ugly word for an ugly phenomenon: the furring of the arteries of a political system. I don't think it's uncharitable or sectarian to suggest that we are long past that point in Wales.

The problem has not been, as is sometimes said, a lack of ambition. The targets that have been set from time to time have been bold and laudable: achieving an average income of at least 90% of the UK average by 2010, being among the top 8 European countries for cancer survival by 2015, or the top 20 worldwide in the PISA education rankings by next year. The problem has been not the aims, but the lack of the vision and leadership necessary to achieve them. When ministers and priorities changed, the targets were quietly dropped.

Those with a sentimental attachment to the Labour Party may hold out hope that it will be possible to renew Welsh Labour from within. I wish them luck. But all the evidence suggests parties only ever renew themselves in Opposition. A country's only hope for renewal after decades of decline is not a change in the leadership of a party, it's a change in the party of leadership.

I like Jeremy Corbyn. In Parliament he was a personal and political friend. It's good to hear that he is about to issue a long-awaited apology regarding Labour's deception on Iraq. But surely it's not Jeremy who should be apologising but the Shadow Defence Secretary and Shadow Foreign Secretary he's appointed to his Cabinet, who approved these illegal wars. Or a Shadow Secretary of State for Wales who voted four times against an inquiry into the Iraq War.

Progress on the path to redemption should always be celebrated, of course. Ten years ago Labour's Cabinet was led by war criminals, now they just have Lord Falconer of Thoroton – a war criminal's advocate, apologist and friend, a perfect choice for Shadow Justice Secretary – the man who convinced the then-Attorney General to change his legal advice.

I say this to Jeremy in comradely fashion: I wish you luck in England. England needs rescuing from the forces of conservatism that have engulfed it. But Wales is another country, with its own politics and its own problems: and the top of that very long list is the failure of your party. The moment you pass through that Severn Tunnel on your monthly procession through Wales, you are not the head of an anti-establishment party: your backward-looking, power-driven, tribalist Labour Party is the very essence of the political Establishment in Wales. You are the status quo; it's we who are the change.

Even the Labour Party agrees that the Labour Party in Wales is a shambles. Ann Clwyd says the Welsh NHS is in dire crisis. Paul Murphy says Valleys schools are no longer producing the kind of good-quality Oxbridge applicants – or matching socks, silk ties and handkerchiefs – they were when he was a boy. You see, on the perpetual training pitch of Welsh democracy, Labour doesn't just field the Government First XV, it provides the Opposition, too – so they win even when they lose. And don't worry about the nuclear button, Jeremy *bach*, that's one bit of devolution Carwyn's in favour of: give him a *cwtsh* and he'll press it for you.

Is this really as good as our Wales will ever get? All of us in Wales in our heart of hearts know – we know, the media knows, the Civil Service knows, the people of Wales know – that we need to change our country. And to change our country, we need to change the government. And to change its government, Wales needs to change its vote. Nothing would shake up the lazy, amoral, unforgivable complacency of our policy and political establishment more than these four simple words: First Minister Leanne Wood.

If you think this is the stuff of dreams, take a look at Alberta in Canada, which in May this year saw a 44-year unbroken term of office by the Conservatives overturned by a New Democratic Party caucus that went from 4 seats to 53. Change, my friends, sometimes comes like an avalanche. The tipping point is now. The leadership is ready. The leadership is willing. The leadership is able. The country is waiting. *A Chymru'n dechrau ar ei hymdaith* – Wales is on its way. Let's Go.

23

There is nothing wrong with Wales that Wales cannot put right

Plaid Cymru Spring Conference, Llanelli
– March 2016

I HAVE DEVELOPED something of a reputation of starting my speeches with historical references. It's a habit I perhaps learned from Gwynfor Evans, from Gwyn Alf Williams, from John Davies, from Hywel Teifi Edwards. We are a party of historians in a nation of historians. Because for us Welsh, the only monuments that we could erect to remind ourselves that we were not dust to the wind were the stories we told each other.

But this year of 2016 is different. This year, the challenge is not to remember but to *be* history, to *make* history, to *shape* history. The challenge for us is not to be passive bystanders at our own funeral but the active agents of our own regeneration.

A hundred years ago, railway workers in this town took control of the level crossings on the Great Western Railway. 80 years before that, the Daughters of Rebecca occupied the toll booths on the Carmarthenshire turnpike. They held the junction points of history in their own hands for a few brief moments, and risked their lives in the process. It's through their struggle and those that followed that we are in the fortunate position as a people that we now find ourselves. For the next nine weeks, the levers of our future lie in our own hands.

We can build the road, lay the track, chart the course of a future that is better than the past. We can make the decisive change in direction that previous generations could only yearn for. It is a historic and heavy responsibility. And it is a responsibility this Party is determined not to shirk.

It's nine weeks out and not a vote has been cast, but I think we can confidently make one prediction. Labour will lose in May. And they deserve to lose because they have already lost any sense of direction, any scrap of creativity, of vision, of drive. They have put us at the bottom of the league for prosperity, for wages, for literacy, for numeracy and science.

I have a particular liking for quotations. You can learn a lot from the wisdom of others. Try this one out for size:

> The first wonder of the world is the mind of a child... Yet we
> are thirty-fifth in the world league of education standards today
> – thirty-fifth. They say 'Give me a boy at seven, I'll show you the
> man at 70.' Well, give me the education system that is thirty-fifth in
> the world today and I will give you the economy that is thirty-fifth
> in the world.

That was Anthony Charles Lynton Blair in his Leader's Speech to the 1996 Labour Party Conference, the last one before he turfed out John Major. Well, in Wales today, 35th place – which Labour said then was a terrible indictment of a failing Government – ranks above us in the same PISA league table. We are 36th in science, 41st in reading and 43rd in the world for maths.

No wonder under Labour we are poorer now relative to all our neighbours, British and European, than we were when

169

devolution began. Remember the 'devolution dividend'. Well, we have had devolution drift and decline. We have the highest economic inactivity rate of any part of the United Kingdom. We have 360,000 people in Wales on hospital waiting lists.

Carwyn says, of course, that he is only halfway through his decade of delivery. And that's true enough. The problem is, the decade's the 1970s. We are going backwards, not forwards, as a nation. What monuments might there be to mark Carwyn's legacy in another five years' time? The closure of Port Talbot, and of Trostre? Steel towns without steel? An airport without passengers? An NHS without doctors? Young people without a future? A nation without hope?

As a party Labour's not just stale, you know, it's sour. Look at the venom and the vitriol of the Labour Party here in Carmarthenshire – the most dishonest political campaign that I can remember in over 30 years in politics, cynically attacking the policies that they agreed to while still in power while disavowing the mess they left as their legacy.

So much for the kinder, gentler politics, eh? Well, what you sow, you shall reap. As students of the modern game of rugby will know, those who engage in foul play will land themselves in the sin bin soon enough. You carry on with your lies, your deception, your personal attacks. Show the people who you are, and we'll do the same, with our heads held high.

I say this to Labour: you are better than this. The party of Jim Griffiths, Nye Bevan and Cledwyn Hughes is better than this. It may be that only through the flames of the furnace of defeat will you discover the mettle of which you were once made. We want better than this. Wales needs better than this. A Wales that can win, not a Wales that can't win, won't win, will never win because it labours under the unbearable complacency that is Carwyn.

We still have freedom of movement in Europe, so we can see with our own eyes how we are falling behind our European neighbours year by year. We can see their higher standards of living, their quality of education, their investment in public transport. And we ask ourselves, what's wrong with Wales? Well, there is nothing wrong with Wales that Wales cannot put right. We have simply put our faith in leaders that have failed us, but the choices we have made can be unmade. We can choose change. If we decide, if we act, then we will change.

Take Wallonia, the French-speaking region in Belgium, similar to us in so many ways. A Celtic people called strangers in their own land, like us they were a powerhouse of the industrial revolution, rich in coal and steel. Like us, they have faced the huge challenge of economic change. But they have embraced that challenge with gusto. Their socialist Government came up with a Plan – they even called it a Marshall Plan, like the one after World War II – to transform their economy from one founded on heavy industry to one fuelled by enterprise, innovation and creativity. They built their plan on six key sectors or poles of competitiveness. And this plan of theirs is delivering. Ten years ago we Welsh earned €2,000 more per person than the Walloons; now we earn €2,000 per person less.

We had a strategy targeted at six key sectors (down from fourteen under Labour) – Ieuan Wyn Jones set it out in 2010. Labour put it back up to nine, and added seven enterprise zones. No wonder even business is confused. The difference between success and failure in business and the economy – and I know from experience – is focus.

Under this Government there is no focus, no clear set of priorities, no strategy, no sense of direction. Since Labour came to power in Cardiff Bay we have been overtaken economically by Portugal, Slovenia, Malta and the Czech Republic. We're level pegging now with Estonia. Some people are talking about leaving Europe. Well, it would be nice if we could catch up. To paraphrase the great Winnie Ewing – stop the world, we want to get on.

We are a talented country. Let no-one doubt what Wales can achieve. Hands up who has a smartphone. (That's about two thirds of those of you that are still awake.) Two thirds of those phones and every smartphone in the world will be run using compound semiconductors made by a Welsh company, IQE – envisioned here, born here, headquartered here. It's not just our own history but our future and our fortune, too, that we can make here in Wales.

We'll establish a National Innovation Body to create that future economy, a new-model development agency to sell Wales across the world, a Bank of Wales to back our businesses, an Infrastructure Commission to lay the foundations of our prosperity not just in one corner of our country, but throughout the land, led not by a Costa Bureaucratica in Cardiff Bay but by a new partnership between people, from every sector and walk of life, who have the knowledge and experience we need and the ordinary commitment that each of us can give to our country. We will create a sense of national mission the likes of which we have not seen in generations – to educate the young, to care for the old, to invest in and for each other.

We'll create a National Citizen Service worthy of the name, for all our young people to have the chance to build up their country – not just to give back but, after they go away, to come back and use for Wales' benefit the knowledge and the skills they have learned. And we will guarantee a job for each and every one of them. Let no-one say that Wales cannot be a land of opportunity. We will create those opportunities together.

There is not one ounce of me that will ever do my country down, nor fail to celebrate any of its little victories. When niche manufacturers come to Wales, I am the first to say my hallelujahs. But I don't want to quench my thirst for good news at the odd oasis in a desert of despair. We will know that we have achieved our dream for our country, my friends, when Wales is no longer surprised by success. What we must bury is the idea of inevitable decline that Leanne referred to yesterday, the toxic myth of inescapable failure because of our national inadequacy. The inadequacy is one of leadership, a monoculture of ideas ranged against a multiplicity of problems. The first step we must take in Wales' liberation is to shatter the single-party mentality of this failed Labour state.

There is nothing inevitable about the outcome of the next few weeks. Every one of us will have a part to play in the great dream that is about to unfold – every campaigner, reporter and citizen. The National Assembly election is the true referendum on which the fate of our nation rests. Mr Cameron and Mr Corbyn disagree, of course. Europe to them is more important than Wales, which is why we are fighting this election in the shadow of an English Civil War being waged to decide who gets to be the next Tory Prime Minister.

Who knows what might happen the morning after June 23rd. We may find by the stroke of an English pencil that we Welsh – a nation founded by a Spanish-born Roman legionary, home to the last Roman monument in the western world – will wake up to find we're no longer European. We will thankfully, at least, still wake up Welsh. As a country, though, we must wake up to the discomforting fact that we risk being crushed between the twin cogs of conservatism: the conservatism of a lame-duck Labour Government, which will lose the election but try to linger on, and a right-wing rump of ex-Tory UKIPers and Eurosceptic, devo-sceptic Tory/UKIP wannabees, clad in camel hair and tweed, their fashion from the 1950s, their economics from the 1930s and their politics from the Stone Age.

We live in a time of crisis – economic, political, moral – the scale of which we haven't seen since Munich smashed the League of Nations. In 1989 I was living in Germany. I was there the night the wall came down. I wasn't on the border between East and West, I was on the Franco-German border in the Saarland, which changed hands four times in four decades of European war. It was the right border to be on that night. I will never forget seeing young French men and women and young Germans embracing each other with tears in their eyes and hope in their hearts that we could live in peace together in what Mikhail Gorbachev famously called our common European home. Well, it is our home still, it is our peace to defend, and we in Wales will fight for it too.

Of course, for all our history of radicalism, our culture of tolerance, our optimism about the future, we in Wales are not immune to the dark forces that the gathering crises of our times are unleashing. There is, though, a particular irony in the fact that Wales, the sick man of Europe, the poorest nation in the entire north and west of this continent, is being invited to switch off its own life-support machine. In the interest of the United Kingdom's independence, apparently we Welsh must do our bit for Queen and Country by quietly committing suicide. The contempt in which we are held is perhaps highlighted by the fact that a party whose biggest gripe is immigrants coming here and stealing our jobs is sending political refugees rejected even by Tory England to claim political asylum and benefits here in Wales. I have been advised that I cannot mention any UKIP candidate by name as they are notoriously litigious – though I cannot for the life of me see how you can sue twice for being called a liar and a thief.

But let not our politics be driven by hate, but by love: love for the land and the people we call Wales, but love also for all of humanity and the planet that is our common home. Sometimes it feels easy to love Wales – driving through the Brecon Beacons, cheering on a winning Welsh team. What is more difficult to love is the more prosaic, the day-to-day and sometimes harsh reality of our nation. To paraphrase Gwyn Alf Williams, we can only truly love Wales if we can put our hands on our hearts and say we love Llanelli bus station in the rain.

What is Llanelli but Wales in miniature? Wales caught here in a teardrop, in a raindrop. Wales is a thousand Llanellis – are we all to be dust in the wind? Working people here in Llanelli, in Wales, in Britain, in Europe have been the raw material for other people's history, other people's battles, other people's wars. It's time we made our own history, built our own country, forged our own future in this furnace of victory. We are a party with a purpose, a movement with a mission, with values from our yesterday and a vision for our tomorrow.

In this week we can perhaps invoke the spirit of Dewi Sant, our patron saint but perhaps in today's Wales a divisive figure: the son of an immigrant who spent at least a few years as a refugee in what is now France. In facing a party that has long been impregnable, we will need to conjure up reservoirs of energy and armies of volunteers, and more converts than the 1904 revival. But don't be daunted. Think like Dewi, wading through the cold mountain stream. In the words of the poet:

> He will not die, he will not run away, he will not exhaust
> He will not fade, he will not fail, he will not bend, he will not
> tremble.

And the victory, my friends, will be Wales'.

[Adam Price was elected AM for Carmarthen East and Dinefwr on 5 May 2016]

24

A new dynamic: rising to the challenge of change

Keynote Speech,
Assembly Election Campaign,
Cardiff Metropolitan University – 2016

I THINK IT was Churchill who said that a speech should only have one point, but Cabinet ministers were allowed three. As a recently appointed Shadow Cabinet minister, I am going to split the difference and allow myself two major points, one about the machinery of government and one about finance, the fuel on which the machine runs. But in a sense, what lies behind both of these is the same underlying idea, that the 'how' of government is often more important than the 'what'. Or indeed the 'who'. Policies and personalities in government often founder on something much deeper, which is the capacity of the system as a whole to effect change, whatever the change is and whoever the change-maker. We need a new dynamic, a new way of working, across government and between government and citizen, if we are to get Wales moving.

Governments at their best can achieve great things. John F

Kennedy famously set a goal for the United States in 1961: to land a man on the Moon and bring him back safely to Earth by the end of the decade. Now, that was what you call a decade of delivery. All the more remarkable given that for him, it was achieved largely posthumously.

Wales has had its own moonshots since the dawn of devolution. There was the goal of closing the economic gap with the UK average to 90% of GVA per capita by 2010. There was the goal of being in the top 20 PISA world education rankings by 2016. There was the goal of achieving 5-year cancer survival rates equal to the best in Europe by 2015. All very ambitious targets, straining at the outer limits of the possible, like Kennedy's New Frontier. But these were great goals which were never met, and the failure to meet them was not marked by a single resignation statement or even an explanation. They were just quietly dropped.

The purpose of this speech is not to lay bare the inadequacies of the current administration. But there are too many of them to be coincidental. Our economy and our education system have declined relatively under devolution, and the most we can say for our health service, despite diverging radically from our near neighbour's, is that it is no better and no worse – though our waiting times are indeed the worst of all the four nations. Over the last ten years, most parts of our country have seen one or other core public service in special measures, a sobering reminder of a system in dire crisis.

Any incoming government of any hue needs to understand the underlying reasons for this systemic failure if it is to have any hope of success. Simply changing the faces around the Cabinet table or the policy papers on it would condemn us to another five years of relative failure, which if we set the bar low enough, of course, can seem like a form of success. The core problem is that government in Wales has become good at the wrong things and bad at the right things. Good at avoiding blame when things go wrong, and keeping ministers out of trouble. Good at defending the status quo. Good at adding management layers and numbers of staff. Bad at basing policies on evidence. At managing resources efficiently. At innovating, reforming and improving service delivery. At being accountable. It's a long list.

To be fair, the Welsh Government faces the same generic problems that governments are facing throughout the democratic world. But there are some unique features to the Welsh Government's predicament which are of their own making. And they flow from a number of conscious decisions:

- The decision to adopt a strong departmental model with a weak centre – the so-called polo-mint government.

- The decision to shut down executive agencies outside of Government – the so-called Bonfire of the Quangos.

- The decision to oppose the kind of market mechanisms embraced in England and North America – so-called clear red water.

Add those three metaphors together – and you get a ring of hot water, which is presumably Wales going down the plug-hole. Let's take each of them in turn and hear what Plaid Cymru, the Party of Wales, is proposing to put in their place.

The term 'silo government' is such a familiar concept to us now that it has become a cliché. The Welsh Government operates as a series of semi-autonomous republics rather than a strategically coordinated state. It is almost self-evidently true that this must have disastrous consequences for outcomes in a world of complex problems whose roots and resolution don't fit neatly demarcated departmental boundaries. A failure to coordinate misses the opportunity to achieve the synergies that any truly comprehensive transformation requires. One has the distinct impression that even when Labour governs alone, ministers hardly talk to each other – and Carwyn only talks to Edwina as he is frightened of her, probably with some justification. The S4C political drama *Byw Celwydd*, in which there are discussions and even votes in Cabinet, is clearly a work of fiction.

The solution to this problem we have known for long time, and indeed the Welsh were in the forefront of those particular innovations. It was 100 years ago that David Lloyd George first created a central organising machine for the Westminster Government, a Cabinet Secretariat – the nucleus of today's Cabinet Office, which employs 2,000 people and is the motor of the UK's Ship of State. There have been some attempts at coordination. The Delivery Unit of six civil servants set up at the beginning of this term and the slightly beefed-up First Minister's Department set up subsequently, partly in response to Gerry Holtham's stinging rebuke which was the source for the polo-mint quip. But these seemed to be modelled on Lloyd George's other innovation, the so-called "garden suburb" of half a dozen key advisors, a third of them Welsh, so called because they were hosted in the garden of 10 Downing Street. This was the seed of the move from government by Cabinet to government as a sort of medieval court, complete with courtiers as gatekeepers to power and very little in the way of collegiate discussion or collective responsibility. Tony Blair moved the Suburb to the Sofa, and the result was the war in Iraq.

We've managed to avoid the pitfalls of centralising power too much in the hands of a single person: the First Minister of Wales is the only one without a residence, and the lights of Tŷ Hywel's 5th floor seldom shine much after 6.00 p.m. This is either a King without a Court, or a Court without a King. It's difficult to say, but the phenomenon of petty fiefdoms and personal rivalries blocking a more strategic unity of Wales as a whole would be pretty familiar to the medieval Prince and early legislator the building is named after.

The answer is to do what almost every other government in Europe does, and create a strong central coordinating office at the heart of government, a centrally empowered Cabinet Office – answerable to the First Minister and staffed by ministerial appointees – leading strategic delivery, alongside a strong Welsh Treasury led by a Finance Minister with wider responsibility for transformational change. We can further remove the scourge of departmentalism by doing what the Scots have done – disempowering the departments, adopting instead a more functional and strategic approach.

If the first problem in the Welsh Government is that they don't talk to each other, the second is that they have very little that is interesting to say. The abolition of executive agencies was, in retrospect, the wrong decision at the wrong time for the wrong reason. Yes, some agencies had not fully adjusted to the new democratic era, but that could have been addressed by a change in the culture of accountability.

In Wales we have sucked power into the Centre, with a Welsh Civil Service as large as Scotland's, which has almost twice the population. Centralising power in the Civil Service can work as a model of government under certain conditions. But the so-called Napoleonic model requires a pool of technically brilliant, highly capable public service leaders. In France they churn them out factory-style in the École Nationale. Under Rhodri Morgan there was talk of creating an integrated Welsh Public Service to widen the reservoir of talent and a Civil Service College to feed it. However, both these laudable ideas were implemented half-heartedly. As is so often the case, we willed the end without willing the means.

The Bonfire of the Quangos might have heralded a new modus operandi, ending the disconnect between practice and policy, service and strategy – but we have seen precious little of that in reality. You would be hard-pressed to find many ex-teachers among the hundreds of officials in the Welsh Education Department. There has been sporadic policy innovation under certain ministers – e.g. Jane Davidson and the heroic effort to introduce Finnish-style learning-through-play.

There has been no shortage of strategies. But there was no strategy, no structure, no theory at the level of the Government as a whole. What we ended up with was a Napoleonic-style system staffed by British Civil Servants trying to deliver Scandinavian policies. Generalist civil servants in the British tradition, who don't know anything in particular – not by accident or omission, but by design. The string of recent embarrassing schoolboy errors – the undervaluation of the land, the overvaluation of Cardiff Airport – are unlikely to have happened in the days of the Land Authority for Wales or indeed the Welsh Development Agency (for all its inadequacies), organisations that had people with relevant experience at the helm. So reliant is the Government these days on external advice, it frequently finds itself getting things badly wrong, as happened with the fiasco over the real costs of the Black Route for the M4 Relief Road. Where experts are brought into government from outside, they are often moved to other departments after a couple of years, as this is the only way they can achieve promotion.

Instead of the Napoleonic model, we should have adopted the small-country, Nordic model of a smart, efficient central state orchestrating a wider system, where detailed strategy and delivery is the work of properly empowered executive bodies, with strong professional competence and technical expertise, democratically accountable but with the autonomy and agility needed to improve the quality and speed of decision-making. Carwyn Jones has dismissed this as Plaid wanting to set up more committees. In fact, it's the opposite of that. If the Tories had their Quango state, Labour has its pro-bonocracy.

This Government has a veritable army of committees, councils and commissions. I know, as until very recently I chaired one of them: the Innovation Advisory Council for Wales. Indeed, the Williams Report, ironically a Commission itself, documented the core function that these advisory bodies play in the structure of governance in Wales. One of the key recommendations of the IACW was that we needed to move from a purely advisory council to an executive National Innovation Body in order to achieve the laudable objectives set out in the Welsh Government's Innovation Strategy. We have excellent strategies in so many areas, but the theory of change that we are currently operating by is for the Assembly to create a statutory duty for someone else to do something and then create a Commissioner or an Ombudsman to report back to the Government on why that is not being done. If there was a Nobel Prize for strategy and scrutiny, Wales would be world famous – it's just what happens, or doesn't happen, in between that is the problem. This is a Government which is trying to steer the country when it has forgotten how to row.

Local knowledge is a form of expert knowledge as well. So alongside the delegation of decision-making power we need internal devolution within Wales. Regional government has emerged within Wales by default in recent years and that needs to be given a consistent institutional form if we are to realise the benefits of a tier that is small enough to be sensitive to local needs but large enough to develop true economies of scope. Finding the right form for decentralised authority has been the Holy Grail of Welsh politics from the *cantrefi* of the Middle Ages to the Counties of 1974 or 1996.

Our solution is not to abolish the existing councils but to use them as the building blocks of a new system of regional government made up of combined authorities led by directly elected mayors. These regional bodies will take over the primary healthcare and public health responsibilities of the local health boards that local government lost under the Heath Government, effectively ending the so-called Berlin Wall between health and social care. In everything from transport to health, social care, education and the economy, a national government in Wales will have powerful regional partners with the capacity to effect change, while maintaining local accountability.

The final question is how we can catalyse innovation and improvement without resorting to the blunt instrument of the market. The rejection of privatisation and marketisation as a simple solution to inertia and inefficiency in the public sector is correct. Competition cannot work as a very effective tool in most of Wales, where urban notions of choice simply don't apply. But what we have signally failed to do is to put an alternative system in place to drive the service improvement necessary if we are to meet the financial challenges that we will inevitably face of delivering better outcomes at lower cost.

There are two baskets of solutions that we will adopt. One is the power of information. As the old adage goes, you can't manage what you can't measure. The Welsh Government has generally rejected the sort of league-table approach adopted in England because it's tainted with the marketisation brush. We do have 243 indicators for the Programme of Government, but they are neither detailed enough to be of use to an individual citizen nor high-level enough to give a sense of overall success or failure. It is a case of hitting the target but missing the point. If we are to improve as a nation, then we need to tap into the collective intelligence of the entire nation. That means throwing open the data-warehouses of Government to allow citizens and companies and social innovators to trawl this vast wealth of information, giving us better accountability, better efficiency, and perhaps the seeds of a new industry.

We've just seen the creation of the first billion-dollar open-data company. We could be at the forefront of this in Wales. We have in south Wales – in ONS, the IPO, the DVLA and Companies House – four of the biggest data-stores of Government in the UK. It was great to see the announcement of the new Data Science Campus in Newport last week. We could be a world-leader in smart government. So we will commit to the principles of Open Government, including the proactive release of all Government information – not just Cabinet decisions, but records, reports and datasets in accessible formats for reuse for any purpose by anyone.

We'll simplify the yardstick of success to three key objectives for the next decade, our Three by Ten:

- Slashing the economic gap between Wales and the UK by 10% by 2026 and achieving parity a decade later.

- Saving 10,000 lives by cutting avoidable deaths by 25% by 2026.

- Achieving a top-ten place for Wales in Europe in all five PISA rankings within a decade.

These are ambitious goals. They will require radical reform which goes far deeper than the structural change of reorganisation. Culture eats structure and strategy for breakfast. We have inherited an attitude of mind from the days of the Welsh Office, more fitted to administration than to innovation. A culture that is cautious, conservative and risk-averse. 'Nobody gets sacked for purchasing IBM' seems still to be the mantra of Cathays Park – even though, of course, nobody buys IBM any more.

We want Wales instead to leverage its small-country advantage – big enough to scale beyond the local but small enough to be manageable – to become the pre-eminent global test bed for public service and economic innovation.

We need to create a new type of leadership in the Welsh Public Sector. So we will give to Wales our own version of the École Nationale – or indeed the Kennedy School, where I had the privilege of studying – a new National Academy of Government, a full post-graduate degree-awarding institution focusing particularly on the governance challenges of small nations and city-regions. It will inherit the functions of the current public-service leadership body Academi and create a world-class cohort of public-service leaders and managers. It will teach new approaches to improving public-sector bureaucracy and organisation, including public-service innovation, service design, behavioural economics and digital delivery.

The Finance Ministry needs to be part of a new, dynamic public sector – no, that need not be an oxymoron. We will invest in an Innovation and Intrapreneurship Fund to invest in more innovative ideas – from public-sector workers, researchers, entrepreneurs and citizens – which, yes, have a higher risk of failure, as that is part and parcel of the innovation process – but which potentially collectively carry with them the promise of transformational change.

The Finance Ministry should also be innovative in the use of the limited tax powers we have. We are in an economic rut as a nation, and to prise ourselves out of that rut we must pull hard on two levers at once: the lever of redistribution and the lever of renewal. We have it in our power to radically reform the most regressive tax in these islands – a legacy of the Thatcher period, the grossly unfair Council Tax, which levies four times as much (as a proportion of wealth) on the poorest as on the richest. That is not the Welsh way, and we will take steps to address that injustice.

We will reform the Council Tax to make it fairer for those in the least expensive properties, cutting the annual liability for three quarters of all taxpayers, equal to a reduction of £400 a year for those in Band A. Those in the highest bands will pay more, an average of 20% more phased in over a number of years, with exemptions for those who are asset rich but income poor, and a new Welsh Middle Rate of income tax, lower than the current rate, to partially compensate. The key word here is 'partially'. Because let's be clear, this change does shift the burden onto the broadest shoulders. That may not be the Osborne way or the Tory way. But it's the right way, it's the Welsh way and it's the way we shall adopt. We will help first-time buyers by raising the threshold at which stamp duty is levied from £125,000 to £145,000, removing over half of all buyers from this tax altogether.

Alongside the lever of equality we also need the lever of enterprise. Three years ago we were the first party to respond to Brian Morgan's review on business rates with a radical package of business-rate reductions, taking 74% of all eligible businesses out of business rates altogether. Today I can announce that we plan on going further. This will mean that Wales will move from having the highest rates for small business to the lowest, giving us a new competitive edge in the battle to attract, retain and motivate the business founders of tomorrow. The new Middle Rate of business rates, too, will make Wales a more attractive location for the entrepreneur, the engineer, the doctor and the dentist – because the inward investment most vital to our future is talent.

This is the new dynamic. A new synthesis between the social democratic values of old and the enterprise, innovation and creativity of a new generation. A country of collective intelligence, to which all of us can contribute and from which all of us will gain. A new government will not by itself mean a new Wales. A new Finance or First Minister will not mean a new Wales. A New Wales means governing anew. That is the challenge of change.

25

This year of serial disappointments will not extinguish our hope

Plaid Cymru Autumn Conference, Llangollen – 2016

CONFERENCE, *DIOLCH*, *DIOLCH*. Thank you all for being here and for everything you do for the Party and for this country. Thank you, each and every one of you, for your service.

There is one person in particular I would like to thank. I have known Leanne Wood for so long I was actually there when she first experienced pasta. She said it could catch on, and she was right on that, as on many things. I have had the pleasure of getting to know so many people who have given their lives to this Party, stalwarts whose years of service are the real bedrock upon which the Party is built. But there are few people I have ever known that have given more than Leanne Wood. She gives her all, day in, day out, in good times, in difficult times – and managing the egos of politicians is difficult even at the best of times – and throughout it all she is there for us, for the

Rhondda, for Wales, for the people. She deserves our gratitude, our commitment and our 100% support.

And speaking of leaders, I'd also like to thank Owen Smith for the red tie I'm wearing – now the Labour election is over he won't be needing it any more.

I have been given that difficult task of presenting the last speech from a Plaid Cymru platform in what has been a year of serial disappointments. You could say this was our generation's *'blwyddyn y pla'* ('year of plague'), to use Gwyn Alf Williams' phrase – because not since 1979 have we faced such a triad of dejection. The Labour Party imploding on the UK stage but somehow limping over the victory line here at home. The vote against Europe. The election of an unapologetically right-wing Tory Prime Minister, egged on by the Murdochite press. To paraphrase another Tory from gentler times, you've never had it so bad.

But you know, in times like this when you feel a sense of desolation, it's always good to get some historical perspective. 1416, six hundred years ago this year, was the year Owain Glyndŵr – who first declared himself Prince of Wales in Glyndyfrdwy, just a few miles up the road from Llangollen – is thought to have died. A man whose birthplace was razed to the ground, who regained his nation's independence only to see it once more lost, his family disinherited, dead or dispersed and his countrymen and women brutally punished through the aptly named Penal Laws. If you think this year's Wales Bill is deficient, you should read the Wales Act passed by Westminster in 1402. One tradition has Glyndŵr being harboured by his daughter Alys at Monnington in Herefordshire, disguised as the Scudamore family chaplain, who may even have been the poet we know as Siôn Cent. In his most famous poem, Siôn Cent contrasts the legendary glories of Wales past with the desperate travails of the Wales around him. But he ends with these words: *Gobeithiaw a ddaw ydd wyf* – my hope is on what is to come.

Whether or not those were the words of Glyndŵr himself, they were certainly the words of someone who breathed the same air, thick with the dust of defeat and a world at large brought low by the Plague. *Blwyddyn y pla* indeed. But even at this darkest hour, the poet could summon up the courage to declare, 'My hope is on what is to come.' That is the courage that we need now. We live in a world and a Wales in pain. If we don't know that, we know nothing. From the charred hiding holes of Aleppo, to the trafficked children of Calais, to a world 72 of whose countries are at war, to the children of our future, who risk suffering environmental catastrophes as terrible as a thousand Aberfans. In this divided and divisive kingdom we have a Tory Party that is moving so far and fast to the right it is rendering UKIP as superfluous as that party did the BNP. These are dark times. Let no-one deny it.

But we will not let the darkness envelop us. It will not extinguish our hope. As they go low, so too will we go high, reaching for the light of a new dawn, a new day in which the future will be better than the past, not some devalued pound-shop imitation of the 1950s, nor some tragic re-enactment of the 1930s. No-one should underestimate the challenges we face. To create the Wales and the world we want to see, we will have to tap the deep reservoirs of hope that sustained this nation and its people in times even more desperate than these. It's easy to despair, to give up, to carp from the sidelines, to blame others and criticise, to withdraw into one's own private world.

This world in pain is crying out not for selfishness, but for self-sacrifice. Not for the narcissism of the few but the bravery of the many. Siôn Cent wrote about *geni'r daroganwr* – the birth of the national saviour who would take our pain away. It is a beautiful piece of poetry, but the more prosaic truth is this, there is no saviour singular. The one we have been waiting for is us. And that's the hard message we have to take to everyone in Wales: we can't do this without you. We can't change Wales without you. There is no force or power outside of ourselves that can change our country. Wales can only heal itself it. This Party, the Party of Wales, can only ever be a vehicle for a process that the people themselves must lead.

We are as strong as you decide. If you look with admiration and awe at Scotland and wish that we had that leadership here, then look straight ahead, my friend, into the mirror, because the answer is there right in front of you. It's great to see this hall full, but look over there, there's an empty chair, and another, and another. Until we fill this hall, and bigger halls, and halls throughout the land, then Wales will not become what it could be. The choice is ours. At this time. In this generation. What will become of us as a nation?

At its best, a political party is an army of practical visionaries, a movement of doers and dreamers who together get big things done. The dreamers of 1945 who built my family's council house, the hospital in which I was born, the mine my father worked, the school and university that educated me and gave me hope of a future that is better than the past. The dreamers of July 1966 in front of the Guild Hall – now owned by the people of Carmarthenshire – who built our Welsh schools, our Welsh Parliament and rebuilt our self-respect as a people and a nation. The dreamers fifty years ago when to be gay was to be guilty, and because of whose courage I am now able to fall in love without fear.

We are all dreamers. If we sleep, we dream – though we may not know it. Dreaming is as natural as breathing, as regular as our heartbeat. And yes we have a dream: a dream of a Wales, free and flourishing, a beacon of justice; a land in which poverty, of ambition and of circumstance, could actually be abolished; a country where knowledge flows freely, where long life is not a lottery but a right, where we heat every home by sun, wind and wave, and where, yes, you can travel from the south to the north of your country via a publicly owned railway that does not make a detour into a neighbouring country.

Independence is a state of mind: to turn our nation into

a start-up society – pioneering, reinventing, shaping anew. And that is not some distant dream: the start-up nation begins when we begin to take power, locally and nationally, and show through the breadth and depth of our innovation the new nation that we could yet be.

I've just negotiated 1% of the budget of the Government of our country. We did some important things:

- We began to close the funding gap with the knowledge base over the border.

- We invested in the best diagnostic technology so we can prise ourselves from the bottom of cancer's survival tables.

- We invested in mental health so we can finally build an NHS of the mind and not just the body.

- We reversed the cuts in the arts, in culture and the language because we believe to truly thrive, a society must also have a soul.

If that's what we could do with the 1%, imagine what we could do with the other 99%.

We are a government in waiting, but we're also an Opposition that's working, in the here and now, because we cannot wait until 2021 to mend people's broken lives and wasted potential. Our patriotism and our politics must be prefigurative. We must build tomorrow's Wales today – because tomorrow cannot wait. We'll put in the foundations to build up the national institutions of a new Wales – a national development bank, a national infrastructure commission, a new national language agency – so when in a few short years we take the keys to our own front door as a nation, when we finally lead the national government of our country, there will be levers there which we can pull to drive our nation forward.

By the way, it was great to see David Marquand, the former Labour MP, here yesterday and joining our Party. Contrary to perception, we in Plaid Cymru do not operate a policy of one in, one out. David's father Hilary Marquand wrote one of the finest pieces on regional economic policy ever – *South Wales needs a plan*. Well, 80 years later and south Wales still needs a plan, and so does the west and so does the north. Wales needs a plan. And such is the scale of the challenge and the opportunity, we need to embody the spirit of the famous injunction by the American architect Daniel Burnham:

> Make no small plans, they have no magic to stir men's blood and probably themselves will not be realized. Make big plans; aim high in hope and work... Remember that our sons and grandsons are going to do things that would stagger us. Let your watchword be order and your beacon beauty. Think big.

We could become a country built not on fear but on hope. A country built on belief in the limitless possibility of human creativity. A small country with big dreams, united in the simple common belief that tomorrow will be better than today. As Eleanor Roosevelt – another First Lady who should have been President – said, "The future belongs to those who believe in the beauty of their dreams." Let that be the promise we make our children, the inalienable right of us all to make the most of our lives – not in narrow materialist terms, but in the highest sense to discover and develop our true potential. Independence is the term for that dream of a self-actualised society, where we live the larger lives we are currently denied. Independence must become our moonshot, an outrageous goal so utterly inspiring that we have no choice but to succeed.

I am often asked if I think Wales ever will be independent. I have to say I find it difficult to believe that alone among all the nations of the earth, we alone will never again be free. The real question, and it is the central question to my generation and the generations below, is one brought to us over the mists of time and the airwaves of history: the first words recorded in a radio message over open sea sent by the Italian Guglielmo Marconi and the Welsh engineer George Kemp, from Flat Holm Island to Lavernock Point, from Wales to Wales. The words that were sent were a question: 'Are you ready?'

It's a question for each and every one of us. Are you ready – to take responsibility, to shape your country's future, to imagine a Wales that is not yet but could yet be? Are you ready to be free? Let us all inscribe our answer not in our words but in our deeds in the days, months and years from this day onwards until we see that great tide of light, from Lavernock to Llangristiolus, of a new dawn, a new day, a new nation.

26

A new Wales, a new chance

Plaid Cymru Spring Conference, Newport – 2017

A FULL GENERATION has passed since this nation of ours decided to place its future in its own hands. This was not just a decision to replace one group of men and women with another. This was a decision to create a New Wales, a Wales in which poverty of ambition and circumstance were abolished and a new era of leadership – purposeful, answerable, inspirational and transformational – was placed at the very heart of our constitution and the public life of our nation.

We wanted our country, so long a land of wasted potential, to be instead a land of opportunity. Our hopes, our demands for our country were by no means radical. By all prevailing standards, they were modest. That our children could grow up free from poverty. That the education of our young and care for our elderly was on a par with our nearest neighbours. That we gave the best chances we could at the start of life and the best care possible at life's end.

1997 was – to use that phrase much uttered of late, sometimes on the most curious of lips – a vote for change. Not change for change's sake, but change for a purpose, the founding purpose of any democracy: to lift up the people by the people's own hand. It wasn't a new state we wanted to build so much as a new society, distinguished by social justice, by economic dynamism and cultural achievement and, yes, its tolerance, kindness and love. 1997 ended 18 years of Conservative rule – and that was undoubtedly a liberation. But much more than that, it ended the studied disdain of distance, social and geographic, that flowed from 500 years of being ruled not by our peers, not by our people, but from the gilded mansions of another nation.

Self-government has never, for us, been an end in itself. It was the means to self-advancement, self-improvement, of self-determination to prise ourselves, not individually but collectively, out of the rut of poverty, ignorance and disease into which accident of birth had consigned us, generation after generation. Government by our own people meant, for us, government for the people above all else. A New Wales, a new chance.

I echo here the sentiments of another young man who fought for his country's freedom, though never enjoyed its fruits: Michael Collins. He, more than any, would have savoured that headline from yesterday: 'Unionists lose majority for the first time in the Northern Ireland Assembly'. If they can do it, then so can we. I was surprised to see Guto Bebb naming him as his political hero the other day, with some half-baked analogy between the Irish Free State Treaty and the Wales Bill. I guess they both sparked a Civil War, though in the latter's case it was confined to the Labour Party.

One thing Michael Collins would never have done is join the Conservative Party. A short while before he was killed, he gave one last speech on Building Up Ireland, setting out his vision for the future of his country. Such is its enduring power, I think it deserves to be quoted at length:

> The growing wealth of Ireland will, we hope, be diffused through all our people, all sharing in the growing prosperity, each receiving according to what each contributes in the making of that prosperity, so that the weal of all is assured. How are we to increase the wealth of Ireland and ensure that all producing it shall share in it? That is the question which... will engage the attention of the new Government. What we must aim at is the building up of a sound economic life in which great discrepancies cannot occur. We must not have the destitution of poverty at one end, and at the other an excess of riches in the possession of a few individuals, beyond what they can spend with satisfaction and justification.

That was Ireland on the cusp of freedom over 90 years ago. Today we are more connected through technology than ever before, but we have, as Age Cymru said yesterday, an epidemic of loneliness. We have a wealth of opportunity – this single hand-held device has more computing power than the Apollo spacecraft used 50 years ago to escape from the gravity of this earth and return safely from the Moon. And yet we are confronted continually by evidence of our failure to solve the most basic problems of our everyday lives. We have the highest proportion of children living in poverty of any nation in the UK: one in three. Two hundred thousand lives blighted right at their beginning. We have had since 2010 a statutory commitment to eradicate child poverty by 2020. While poverty has fallen in Scotland and the north-east of England, here it's increased compared to ten years ago, and is set to increase further. And what's the Welsh Government's policy response? To end our biggest anti-poverty programme, Communities First, and put nothing in its place.

25 years ago I wrote a report for a major conference on the future of the Valleys – 'Rebuilding Our Communities' – with Professor Kevin Morgan, who went on, of course, to lead the 1997 Yes Campaign. The depressing fact is that on rereading the report now, it has retained its underlying relevance. Kevin was then a member of the Labour Party, which he has since left. We quoted David Marquand, who was then a member of

the Labour Party, and subsequently left to join us, and was here with us yesterday. All three of us are, I suspect, natural co-operators, progressive pluralists by inclination, striving to find the common ground which can often be our best chance for change. We ended our report with these words:

> If the unpretentious claims of the Valleys – for decent jobs, for better public services and for a clean environment – are to be met, we simply must come to terms with the fact that what we have in common is far more enduring than what divides us here in south Wales.

It's that characteristically Welsh motivation – the disposition to co-operate for the common good of our nation – that brought us together under one banner in 1997 in Yes for Wales, and ten years later in One Wales. It's why we work where we can, even now in Opposition – on the Welsh Brexit Common White Paper for example – to embody the politics of the united front, not that of a broken nation.

But the problem – and I say this in regret as much as in reproach – the problem in all this is glaringly obvious, and that is the Labour Party. This is a party born from the struggle for social change which now propagates, in our country at least, the mindset of social inertia. The First Minister, by temperament and belief, is about as far as it is possible to be from embodying the radical urgency of now. There was a time when, stung by my criticism of bad political posture, he started standing up straight at that lectern in First Minister's Questions. But now he's slouched back into the slow and easy complacency of unchallengeable supremacy. A session at First Minister's Questions is like being enrolled at a really poor quality university, being lectured at but learning nothing. A few weeks ago he proudly told us, arm resting on his rostrum, how he'd first come up with the idea for the Metro at Bedwas Rugby Club. Sometimes if I close my eyes, I can hear him saying to strangers at the bar in the rugby clubs of his retirement: I used to run a country once. Labour in Wales is failing and it will fall. The only question is who will be there to pick up the pieces.

For the future of our nation, at this time, there can only be one answer to that question. It has to be us. Not us in the narrow sense of this Party, but us in the collective sense – represented by this Party – of taking responsibility for our own problems, the solutions to which, as we hold up a mirror to the state of our nation, are quite literally staring us in the face. That task of moving from complainants to controllers of our own fate, authors of our destiny, shapers of our future, begins with the local elections in May. Wales will not be liberated by a mass march in Cardiff, or even a match in Cardiff: it is those small steps you take – down a farmyard lane, up and down a Valleys terrace – and the time you take to listen that will liberate Wales. Brick by brick, the new Wales will be built from the blessed ground up. Governing locally is how we demonstrate to people nationally that there is a better way. That we don't have to accept the inevitability of poverty, disadvantage and decline. That another Wales is not just possible but the urgent imperative of the times in which we live.

We have under-invested for generations in the skills of our young and the care of our elderly. The new tax powers give us new possibilities and we as a nation must now decide on our priorities. So we as a party will ask the people of Wales over the summer how these new powers should be utilised. Should we raise a penny for a purpose – dedicated to transforming our beleaguered NHS? Two hundred million for our schools and colleges could close the gaping chasm of funding per student between Wales and our neighbours. We could, if we chose to, build a health and education system that was equal to the best. We could become the test-bed nation for solving the societal challenges of the next generation.

And in that spirit of innovation I'm pleased to announce we are, as a Group in the National Assembly, about to create an ideas lab focusing on new ideas for our economic transformation, which – given that our guiding inspiration is that new Wales which we have a restless desire to build – we will call Nova Cambria. Nova Cambria, for the Welsh historians among you, was the first attempt to create a new Welsh homeland in south America, some 15 years before Y Wladfa. Led by the visionary Thomas Benbow Phillips from Tregaron, after settling in Brazil the community failed when many of its members, some of whom were colliers from this old county of Gwent, decided to work in nearby mines owned by others rather than attempt to grow their own cotton. There is a something of a metaphor there for the Welsh predicament.

We have long planted the seeds of our hope in distant shores and distant cities. But the hard truth inscribed in the bitter arc of our own history is this: we can only ever build the future of which we dream here in our own land, with our own hands. We don't believe in self-government for self-government's sake, or Opposition for Opposition's sake. We're not here to tear down. We're here to build. So this May let's begin to build that New Wales. Here. Now. Together.

27

A Guggenheim for Wales

The case for a National Gallery
for Contemporary Art – 2018

A DECADE HAS passed since a Welsh Government-commissioned study last recommended that Wales create a National Gallery for Contemporary Art. The sub-prime mortgage crisis in America meant we instead got a sub-prime solution in the form of a new wing for the National Museum's Cathays Park base. The fact that in 2018 Wales has just half a National Gallery and no National Gallery of Contemporary Art at all says more about the culture of our state than the state of our culture. Soon another feasibility study will report, but there's been little debate so far on what kind of new cultural institution we could and should create, or whether we need one at all.

I will lay my cards firmly on the green baize. We have many truly excellent existing galleries – MOMA in Machynlleth, Oriel Mostyn in Llandudno, Oriel Myrddin in Carmarthen, Oriel Davies in Newtown, the Glynn Vivian in Swansea and Aberystwyth Arts Centre (and also artist-led initiatives like G39 in Cardiff, Cyfuno Wrexham, Arcade Cardiff and Colony Projects in Port Talbot), to name but a few. But in terms of what is required in Wales to put art and creativity at the centre of things, these are like seventeenth-century Quaker meeting houses – disparate gatherings of the devoted few – when what we really need is something on the scale of the great cathedrals or the Methodist Revival.

My previous intervention in this debate, five years ago, was to pitch for a Welsh Guggenheim. The unexpected rejection by Helsinki City Council of a well-advanced proposal to build a second European base for the renowned New York arts foundation, I argued, created a unique opportunity for Wales. While the Basques I had been speaking with were quite supportive, when the BBC ran the idea as an almost-done deal I was soon on the receiving end of an almighty put-down by the New York Foundation's Director, Richard Armstrong, declaiming, in a terse email delivered via his spokesperson, "unequivocally that we will not entertain the idea of a Guggenheim in Wales."

The fact, as it later emerged, that Mr Armstrong was involved in then-confidential discussions to revive the Helsinki proposal possibly explained the strength of their ire. A few months later a revised project was approved, an architect appointed... until the Finns changed their minds again and killed the project for good. I wonder whether Mr Armstrong would be quite so unequivocal about Wales now.

But in the subsequent years I've changed my mind about the value of cultural 'inward investment'. The Pompidou, the Louvre, the Hermitage and, within the UK, the Tate and the V&A have all adopted the same branch museum strategy. Which means the Bilbao Effect – borrowing cultural capital from elsewhere to catapult oneself into the big league – is now pretty much nugatory. As Hans Ulrich Obrist has argued, "the most interesting international art institutions will be the ones that succeed in making a stand against the homogenising stances of globalisation, building discourses around local cultures and genius." Expecting a creative organisation from outside to arrive in Wales to solve all our problems is, as former National

Theatre Wales Director John McGrath said in his 2016 Hay Lecture, looking down the wrong end of the telescope.

The starting point in imagining what a National Gallery of Contemporary Art could and should be, therefore, is to dare ourselves to be ourselves. Simply building another me-too monument in Cardiff – build it and it they will come – in a world where every wannabe cultural capital has invested billions in courting Richard Florida's creative class, seems inherently to be a bad idea. The genesis of the National Theatre of Wales, which eschewed a traditional venue-based or touring model to create its own unique idea, a peripatetic laboratory of site-specific work culminating memorably in its inaugural year in the magnificent *Passion of Port Talbot*, shows what might be possible in reinventing the idea of what a national cultural institution could be.

Adapting NTW's idea of the nation – its beaches, forests and factories – as stage could mean seeing the nation as gallery, in the same way that Cardiff Contemporary has turned the city's urban fabric into a mass exhibition space. This could mark a return to the mobile exhibitions that the Arts Council of Wales funded to international acclaim in the 1970s as part of the Art and Society programme, with enigmatic billboards at railway stations on subjects like sex and work, and the German Imperial flag flying controversially above the National Museum to mark the opening series on war. A Welsh take on the Casa FOA festival in Buenos Aires, with a new building every year made over room by room as a showcase for the best in art, design and architecture, could perhaps be repeated every year, Eisteddfod-style, in a different valley, village or city street. There could be a particular emphasis on events as an artistic medium, emulating, for example, Canvas Chicago's *Sub Chroma*, an annual exploration of art and tech with disused warehouses and factory spaces turned into an immersive virtual playground of interactive installations, curated galleries of physical and digital work, music and live performance.

So in a small, decentralised nation like Wales, any truly National Gallery of Contemporary Art must see its mission as being beyond its building. But it will still need a home. At a practical level that's because the visual arts, more than other art forms, are displayed over long periods rather than performed over short ones. In other words, you need a lot of space. And though the culturally democratic idea that art can be anywhere is important, we also need palaces of culture or *Kunsthalle* – to use that wonderfully grand European phrase – where we concentrate art so that we can appreciate it on a scale and intensity above that of our everyday experience. As Tate Modern has demonstrated, these cathedrals of creativity can democratise culture without in any way dumbing down.

If there has to be a building then, as this is Wales, our national conversation will soon focus on where, though the more interesting questions are 'What?' and 'Why?' To some extent, however, these questions are interlocked. Galleries in unexpected places are doing unexpected things because they have to strive more in order to flourish. MASS MoCA is a sprawling complex of converted industrial buildings in a former mill-town in the Berkshires region of Western Massachusetts. Opened in 1999, it is the original template where the later Guggenheim Director Thomas Krens first formulated the ideas that he would use to such to great effect in Bilbao – itself at the time, an ugly, rusting post-industrial hulk of a city, as unlikely a choice for art metropolis as you could imagine.

In any country the capital city will be the obvious place for a new national cultural institution. Cardiff is also a major creative and cultural hub. But because it's so obvious, we should purposely look elsewhere. A strong case, for example, could be made for a rural location for a contemporary art gallery, as Hauser & Wirth's Somerset outpost and the Louisiana Museum of Modern Art, Denmark's most visited gallery, have proven. As the visual arts have become more than just painting – with sculpture, performance and installations alongside digital and video/film – then the white cube of the conventionally urban gallery is just one format in an increasingly diverse art ecosystem that now comprises sculpture gardens, landscaped art parks and courtyarded art environments.

Even in Bilbao, the outside has become at least as important as what's inside. It's the Frank Gehry building itself, its setting and the massive Jeff Koons puppy at its door that are for many the real draw. The importance of vista and the external environment chimes with the landscape tradition in Welsh art, and Welsh thought's wider emphasis on *cyd-ymdreiddiad* – the interpenetration of place and culture. There is more than just a whiff of Frank Lloyd Wright's original vision for his Taliesin schoolhouse in former London art dealer Richard Salmon's ideas for the Gelli Aur estate in Carmarthenshire: a rural salon of transdisciplinary creativity, where artists-in-residence will be literally so in an integrated complex of in-house work/live spaces, the modern equivalent of the artists' colony.

To break the false – and very English – dichotomy between rural Eden and the urban landscape's dark satanic mills first laid bare in Raymond Williams classic study, *The Country and the City*, a Welsh National Gallery of Contemporary Art would do well to have both a rural and an urban canvas. There are lots of interesting potential locations for the latter: Pontypridd (Owen Smith MP's original suggestion of a Tate on the Taff), Swansea (where plans are afoot to regenerate the Hafod Copperworks), or Newport (one of the few cities in the UK to lack any kind of contemporary art gallery) to name just a few.

My current vote for an urban campus, however, for a Museum of Living Art (a much better term in contrasting with the dead art of historical collections, I believe, than 'modern' or 'contemporary') would go to Port Talbot. It is not picture postcard Wales, but it has a certain rough-hewn beauty which makes it a place of pilgrimage to photographers at night, which Fox Talbot – the pioneer of photography and scion of the town's founding family – would no doubt appreciate. As infrastructure in Wales was built around its extractive economy, Port Talbot has among the best transport links of anywhere in Wales. If the Rhondda Tunnel is reopened, its final destination would be here. What better place to build a new Wales, where what we extract is creativity through knowledge.

Art can flourish in out-of-the-way places. The Museum of Old and New Art opened in 2011 by the gambling magnate David Walsh in Hobart, Tasmania has been a massive hit with both critics and the public. Likewise the Crystal Bridges Museum of American Art funded by Walmart heir Alice Walton in Bentonville, Arkansas, or the Benesse Art Site built by Japanese billionaire Soichiro Fukutake that has turned Naoshima Island into a modern art mecca. What is true of all these examples is that they have embodied a certain experimental or pioneering spirit which is about as far away as possible from the carefully curated predictability of the publicly funded institution. MONA's ironic marketing pitch is: "Catch the ferry. Drink beer. Eat cheese. Talk crap about art. You'll love it."

The individuality of these places has a lot to do with the fact that they are funded by visionary individuals (or their foundations) with deep pockets. So one of the main challenges we face is how to compete with that in the context of an austerity-ravaged public sector. Ideally we need a modern Carnegie – not just to fund a building, but to make it an engine of creativity on a global scale. We are, after all, about to place creative problem solving and critical thinking and play at the heart of our education system through the Donaldson proposals. Ironically, the only two nations to do so (Finland and Wales) will be one that rejected Guggenheim and another rejected by them. Imagine we now created our own foundation – who knows, maybe jointly with the Finns – which sought to fire up every child's spark of creativity, so often dulled by the time we reach adulthood. Wales only has about half a dozen billionaires. Perhaps a compelling case could be made to one of them to make Wales the cradle of a post-industrial revolution.

28

A penny on tax will help wake Welsh potential

The Sunday Times, 22 July 2018

WALES IS A small country crying out for big ideas. That was brought home in stark terms last week by the 'farewell letter' of the retiring auditor general of Wales. Auditors are by nature cautious. Huw Vaughan Thomas' valedictory, however, was a rallying call for radical thinking to take the place of the apathy, incrementalism and inertia that dogs Welsh political culture.

It says something about the state of a country when it is the audit office that makes the most compelling case for change. It is the tragedy of Wales' brand of 'weak managerialism' that it aims to be mediocre at everything – and fails even to achieve that. It is time to turn this self-defeating logic on its head and instead ask what we want to be uniquely good at, and then allow that excellence to permeate all we do.

The academic Mariana Mazzucato talks about the power of a mission-driven policy: set a single, stretching goal and then build the interlocking policies to make that happen. The best example of this is President John F Kennedy's determination that the US go to the Moon in the 1960s. So here's a goal for

Wales: while aspiring to be a good place in which to grow old, let us aim to be the best country in Europe in which to be young. In a sense, that goal is implicit in the Wellbeing of Future Generations Act, designed to be the operating system of our politics. Experience, though, suggests otherwise. Health and social care have been sheltered from the worst ravages of austerity for understandable reasons but Welsh schools, colleges and universities, already poor relations of their English counterparts, have seen cumulative cuts that have demoralised staff while gutting the chances of a generation.

It wasn't meant to be this way. Increasing schools' per-pupil spending by 1% above the Barnett block every year was the central idea in First Minister Carwyn Jones' bid for the Welsh Labour leadership ten years ago. His manifesto, *Time to Lead*, should perhaps have been called *Time to Lag* because what we've seen in the "decade of delivery" is a 5% real-terms cut. Investing in education is basically a down payment on the future, which makes our decision to persistently raid the education budget to shore up other spending – including the bloated economy department's obsession with a grant-aid culture – all the more perplexing.

Research funded by the Hodge Foundation into the Welsh predicament looked at factors that could explain economic success in 530 regions worldwide. It found that spending on primary, secondary and higher education was conspicuously the most important. A survey of Welsh companies by the same researchers at Cardiff Metropolitan University cited skill shortages as the biggest constraint to growth.

Offa's Gap – the gulf in output between Wales and the rest of the UK – is largely a problem of productivity. It is no surprise, then, that Professor Calvin Jones, the Cardiff Business School economist, has said the most beneficial action we can take for our economy, our society and our future is to spend an extra £1bn on making the Welsh education system as modern as anywhere else in the world.

So why don't we? A penny for education – a 1p tax increase – would allow us to invest that amount in schools and colleges and universities over an assembly term. Diverting £150m from a flabby economy department could fund £2.5bn in capital through long-term borrowing. We could create innovation campuses throughout Wales, not just in SA1 in Swansea; we could have specialist unis and colleges such as Newport's nascent 'software university'... and we could build up-to-date schools for everyone, not just the lucky few.

We could end the crisis in our education system which has made us the worst in the UK in the Pisa international student assessment. We could make teaching a valued, high-paid, high-skilled profession once more. We could turn further education from Cinderella sector to the high-powered engine of a new European-style vocational system. Wales – which gave the world the first mass adult literacy programme in the eighteenth century and the first comprehensive school in the twentieth – could be the knowledge nation of the coming machine age.

If we are to achieve that ambition, it is our politics that must stop being robotic. Dare anyone be so bold? The prospects are not positive. Welsh politics prefers its policies and leaders tried and tested, not radically experimental, which probably explains two decades of decline.

Cumulative failure, though, always leads to a crossroads where a society is willing to change direction. Wales is at such a crossroads. In the late 1970s when Ireland faced a similar choice between continuing failure or an alternative future, it embarked on a determined programme of Keynesian fiscal expansion. As a macroeconomic policy it was misguided. Because much of the money was invested in education, however, it woke the Celtic tiger.

Whether our own dragon will emerge from its slumber, and how, are the fundamental questions that every would-be leader needs to answer.

29

In politics, momentum
is everything

Western Mail – 14 June, 2011

IN POLITICS, MOMENTUM is everything and there can be little
doubting the fact that Plaid Cymru has slipped into reverse
gear. Becoming the third, not the second, biggest party in
the National Assembly is particularly disappointing, because
that means the landscape of Welsh politics has become less
distinctly Welsh. We now have an Official Opposition – the
Conservatives – which can never form a government since my
Party would never under any circumstances back a Tory-led
coalition. So what advice would I give to Plaid's new chief
executive, about to be appointed over the next few weeks?

Firstly, I think we need a period of calm heads. While the
result was bad, it wasn't as disastrous, say, as that of the Bloc
Québécois, who lost all but four of their 49 seats in the recent
Canadian general election, or that of our Catalan sister party,
Esquerra, which lost more than half its seats as punishment
for participation as a junior party in its version of One Wales,
in coalition with the Socialists in the Catalan Government. So
things could have been worse. Highs and lows are part and

parcel of the pendulum swing of politics. This is particularly true of nationalist movements, bound up as they are with the national psyche that seems to vacillate between euphoria and despair. Plaid needs to heed the sage advice of Israel's Ariel Sharon: stay on the big wheel, as in politics your time will come round again.

This is no cataclysm then. But it is an opportunity to reflect on some deeper issues, which came to the fore during earlier periods of enforced introspection – after the 2005 Westminster election, for example – but remain unresolved.

The first one is the perception that we are a party only for Welsh speakers. This remains our biggest challenge, and there have been repeated attempts to reach out – changing our logo from the mountain peaks of Snowdonia to the more ubiquitous Welsh poppy was an attempt, for example, to achieve a pan-Wales appeal. While the Party's reinvention was partially successful – our vote went up in the next Assembly and European elections – it obviously didn't go far enough. Internal polling by the Party has shown that our level of support among English-speaking women, in particular, is worryingly low. We have to become a truly national party, and the most obvious place to start is the Party's name – reverting to our roots, as it happens: Plaid Cymru must also be the 'Welsh National Party', a party for everyone who lives here.

The second issue we have to confront is the continued confusion over our constitutional policy. We behave – to borrow an analogy from another context – like 'closet nationalists', frightened of people's reactions to who we really are and what we believe. This convinces no-one and leaves us looking weak and even devious, which is worse. It's time we came out and said it: our dream is Welsh independence. For that dream ever to become reality then the biggest problem we must solve is economic. As Gerry Holtham argues in an extremely perceptive piece in the current edition of the Welsh-language monthly *Barn*, we should place our economic policy four-square at the forefront of our political programme.

This will be a major departure for the Party – though it carries with it echoes of an earlier upsurge in the Party's support in the 1970s, when Dafydd Wigley, Phil Williams and Eurfyl ap Gwilym came up with the masterful Economic Plan for Wales, which was to lay the foundations for the creation of the Welsh Development Agency. For most of its history, however, Plaid has tended to prioritise cultural demands. From the 1980s, the Party widened its focus to include social and environmental objectives. Important as these are, they fail to address the single biggest underlying reason why the national movement in Wales is weaker than in Scotland: a concern for our economic viability as a nation. Closing Offa's Gap – the prosperity divide with England – has to become our psychological contract with the Welsh people. If we achieve that, then they may take a second look at the prospects for independence.

Many on both the left wing and the right wing of my Party, for different reasons, either fail to understand or refuse to accept that the fundamental difference between us and the Labour Party is not one of values. We both stem broadly from the same progressive tradition of the European centre-left. The difference is one of aspiration. The incoming Economy Minister, Edwina Hart, for example, sought to lower expectations of what could be achieved on the economic front by a "regional Government on the edge of Europe". Similarly the Labour Government's much-touted emphasis on delivery is in actual fact a recipe for five years of the worst kind of micro-managerialism, a vacuum of inspiration and ideas. Wales needs an alternative to that, and Plaid needs to make clear that its ambition is to provide a non-Labour, left-of-centre alternative government, as the SNP has successfully done in Scotland. That means going into the 2016 and all subsequent elections with a clear commitment that the only government that we will join is one in which we lead. Let's leave the eternal apprentice role to the Lib Dems.

Which leaves us with the question of what to do now on two pressing fronts: that of the question of the Party's leadership and the issue of whether to re-enter the coalition in the interim. As regards the former, I think that Ieuan Wyn Jones is to be commended on providing the Party with the breathing space it needs to put in place all the changes that the incoming new chief executive will, no doubt, want to institute. A leadership election can be a source of renewal, but in the Party's current state I fear it might be something of a distraction. The problems the Party faces are much deeper than one of personnel.

Regarding 'One Wales Two', I can only envisage one prize that is big enough to merit Plaid re-entering government in the short term, and that is a commitment to a commission to consider the constitutional implications for Wales of a Yes Vote in the forthcoming Scottish independence referendum, including a pledge to consult the Welsh people on Wales' future in the wake of Scottish independence. It's tough to argue the case against the right to self-determination. If nothing else, it would be fascinating to see Carwyn Jones try.

30

A wealthy country that lives in poverty (Part 2)

Plaid Cymru Spring Conference, Llangollen – 2018

WE'VE COMFORTED OURSELVES too long by blaming others for our misfortunes. The answer is to take our future into our own hands. And that means taking it out of the hands of the Welsh Labour Government, who can best be described – to use that colourful phrase of the great Irish firebrand P S O'Hegarty – as "a collection of mediocrities in the grip of a machine", the most pathetic and ineffectual one-party state in the history of one-party states. Mediocrity for this Welsh Labour Government is something to be aspired to, and they can't even manage that.

Which is why our nation is crying out for change in 2021. We have to win. Not for ourselves. Not for our Party. Not for the ordinary stuff of political gain. We have to win for Wales, for democracy and for our future. Because if Labour wins again and rules unchallenged for thirty years then everything we have won, everything we have fought for and everything we cherish is at risk. The stakes really are that painfully high.

But we will not create the Wales that we want by simply

railing against the Wales that is. We need to paint a new Wales in the minds of our people with the most vivid brushstrokes of our imagination. Our Imagined Nation. We need to render a vision of what Wales by 2030 could be. A new vibrant, confident, successful nation built on the foundations of two terms of a Plaid Cymru administration. What could we achieve over the course of that decade? What tens of leaps forward could we make by 2030? We will all have our own ideas as to what that progress could be. That is the conversation we want to have now with the Welsh people. But let me start to give a flavour of what might be possible.

- In terms of our national infrastructure, we will want to build a Wales which will connect the north and south of our country with a new national railway line and yes, a national expressway, a digital fibre spine the very equal of Scandinavia and South Korea – and Cornwall even. We will build a national energy grid, with a national energy company connecting locally owned energy-generating companies in every part of Wales.

- We will create an International Wales. A Wales that is an associate member of UN bodies like UNESCO, with its own para-diplomatic strategy, which, in this week of the World Cup qualifiers, has its own cricket team and, yes, if the Faroe Islands succeeds in its application, its own Olympic team too. A Wales that will hold a World Expo for the first time in these islands since Dublin in 1907. A Wales that will build connections to the rest of the world not just through its own airport, but through its own national air carrier, which will create direct connections to the Americas and mainland Europe, as well as to the rest of the UK and the rest of Wales through a network of regional airports.

- Where Theresa May wants to ban plastic by 2042 and

petrol and diesel cars by 2040 –which means no action for a generation – we could pledge to create a clean, green Wales by 2030, by making Wales the pathfinder for ending the use of both. Our country would become the test bed of global innovation.

- By 2030 we could seek to make Wales the most attractive place to be young in Europe – apart from maybe Ibiza in August – by making university education free again for Welsh students committed to studying at home, by building a free, universal and fully bilingual childcare service and by introducing the world's first youth basic income, a guaranteed minimum income for all those in full-time work or education, and a guaranteed job for the un- and under-employed.

- We'll introduce our own national digital parallel currency, alongside the pound, which would allow us creative ways of working round Westminster austerity, increasing local procurement and enhancing the circular economy.

- We will create a National Housing company to build new homes and new towns across the nation to end homelessness completely by 2030.

- We will build up modern public transport systems everywhere in our nation and, step by step, we will make them free for all.

- We will make every school a bilingual school so that by 2030 no child will leave our education system without knowledge of both our languages, and most children will leave with knowledge of three or more.

- We will create a National Care Service funded by general taxation, delivered through local government, free at the point of use.

- And we will end this decade of democracy in action by pledging to organise a national referendum on the constitutional future of our country, which will ask this coming generation where they want Wales to be mid-century, and will certainly include independence as a realistic option. And that is a referendum that at that point in our history we could win, because we will have demonstrated at last what self-government could mean.

But first we have to win an election. And not one but two. And that will take discipline. It will take determination. It will mean putting aside petty differences and personal ambition to serve the common cause. A hundred years ago, politicians in Ireland, Australia and Canada built their independence from the once-mighty British Empire step by courageous step. They had the discipline and determination and selflessness of those that had experienced the tragedy of war. Thank God we have not had to experience that burden. But we need to mirror the depth of their character.

What we need is ten thousand citizens of a republic of the mind, of a Wales already free, who will march together as comrades in a great movement of ideas. Our enemies are poverty, ignorance, disease, cowardice and selfishness. The enemy of those enemies is you, my friends and comrades, and our place is by each other's side. We march shoulder to shoulder, in lockstep together, or we do not march at all. We have many miles to cover and we are surrounded on all sides by cynics and the sounding brasses of the self-important, the self-indulgent, the self-centred. We have to ignore those voices if we are to find our own. The only self there is room for in this movement is self-government.

Are you ready to add your voice to that greatest of all causes? To liberate this nation from poverty, from sickness, from ignorance and timidity? Are you with us? Are you with us? Then let the work begin.

Also from Y Lolfa:

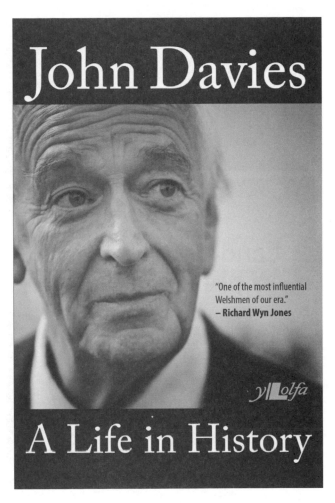

John Davies

"One of the most influential
Welshmen of our era."
– **Richard Wyn Jones**

y Lolfa

A Life in History

£9.99

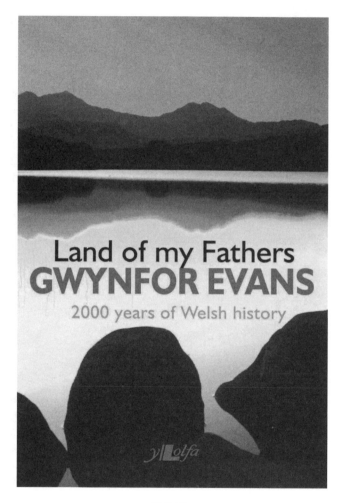

Land of my Fathers
GWYNFOR EVANS
2000 years of Welsh history

y Lolfa

£12.95

Meic Stephens

More
Welsh*lives*
Gone but not forgotten

41 obituaries of eminent contemporaries

y Lolfa

£9.99

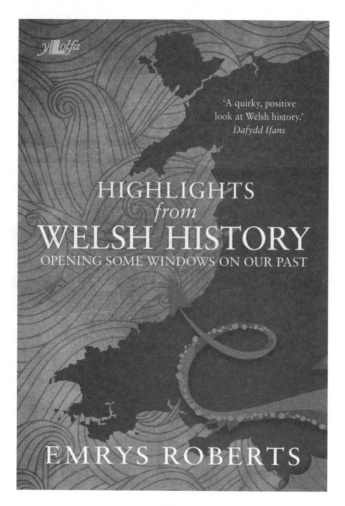

'A quirky, positive
look at Welsh history.'
Dafydd Ifans

HIGHLIGHTS
from
WELSH HISTORY
OPENING SOME WINDOWS ON OUR PAST

EMRYS ROBERTS

£3.99

Wales: The First and Final Colony is just one of
a whole range of publications from Y Lolfa.
For a full list of books currently in print, send
now for your free copy of our new full-colour
catalogue. Or simply surf into our website

www.ylolfa.com

for secure on-line ordering.

TALYBONT CEREDIGION CYMRU SY24 5HE
e-mail ylolfa@ylolfa.com
website www.ylolfa.com
phone (01970) 832 304
fax 832 782

Ask for a print quote!
01970 832 304